SPECTRUM WRITING

CONTENTS

Project Editor: Sandra Kelley
Text: Written by Sandy McKinney and Michael Litchfield
Design and Production by A Good Thing, Inc.
Illustrated by Karen Pietrobono, Anne Stockwell,
Doug Cushman

Things To Remember About Writing

WRITING

- Present the events of a story in a clear order. Use flashbacks to explain how something came to be.
- Use an outline to organize ideas and put them in order for a report.
- State the main idea of a paragraph in a topic sentence. Put the topic sentence at the beginning or end of the paragraph.
- Use sense details to describe people and places.
- Use comparative words, similes, and metaphors to make comparisons interesting.
- Use only facts in an objective article, such as a news story. Express your feelings and opinions in a subjective article, such as an editorial.
- Write persuasively by basing opinions on facts.
- Use a first- or third-person point of view, depending on how much of the characters' thoughts you wish to reveal.
- Choose the genre that best expresses the point of view you want to use: play, poem, short story, essay.

REVISING

- Add adverbs to your writing to tell how, when, and where.
- Use conjunctions to show cause-and-effect relationships and to combine short, choppy sentences.
- Avoid unnecessary or misplaced modifiers.
- Replace vague or general words with specific nouns, verbs, and adjectives.
- Give your paragraphs better rhythm by combining sentences, removing repetitious words, and varying sentence structure.

unit 1

Writing in Sequence

Things to Remember About Writing in Sequence

Sequence tells the order of events.

Writing

- Present the events of a story in the order in which they happened in order to keep the sequence clear.
- Use flashbacks in stories to show how a situation came to be the way it is, or to tell what is happening in a character's mind.
- Use an outline to organize your ideas and put them in sequence before you write a report.
- Organize your outline into main heads, subheads, and details.
- Add more details when you write up the report in order to make the report more interesting.

Revising

- Add adverbs to your writing to give specific information about *how, when*, and *where*.

lesson

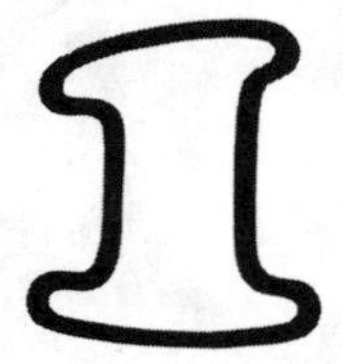

Writing a narrative in sequence

This true story describes a number of events. They took place in a certain order, or **sequence.**

After lunch I went out in back of the barn. I noticed that the fence around the garden had been knocked down. In the potato patch, there was dirt freshly kicked up, and hoof prints were everywhere. Several plants had been uprooted, and the new potatoes had been eaten. I followed the tracks into the western field and found the new cow by the first gate, lying on her side and bloated horribly. You couldn't even see her ribs, the potatoes had made her swell up so—just as yeast makes bread rise. She had trouble breathing, and yank and kick as I might, she wouldn't stand up. I knew then that she would probably die.

A. Briefly list in sequence the events of the story so far. What was the first thing that the person telling the story did? What next? And after that? The list has been started for you.

Went out in back of barn
____

____

____

____

____

B. The story continues below, but the events have been scrambled. Read all the sentences and number them in what you think is the correct sequence.

_____ I stayed with her all night. The next day, when the vet came, he said I had done the right thing.
_____ I ran up to the house and tried to call the vet, but no one answered.

_____ I went back to the cow anxiously. If I did nothing, she would surely die. So I got a knife and a short piece of iron pipe.
_____ With the knife, I made a small cut in the cow's side and eased in the piece of pipe.
_____ The cow recovered. She was a good milker and high spirited. But she never did have potatoes again for supper.
_____ The pipe kept the cut open so that the pressure could escape.

C. Think of some ideas for a true story you could write. What are some interesting things you know about that have really happened? Answer each of the questions below.

1. Have you, or has anyone you know, ever tried to rescue or help out an animal or another person? If so, who rescued whom?

____

____

2. Have you ever been in a situation that was really frightening? If so, what was it?

____

____

3. Has anything recently amused you or made you angry? If so, what?

____

____

4. Think of something else that happened to you or to someone you know that would make a good story. What was it?

____

____

D. From the list of ideas you wrote on the previous page, choose the one that interests you most. Then list in sequence the events that you would want to include if you wrote the story. These are notes for a story, so you don't have to use complete sentences. Just jot down your ideas.

Topic you chose: ______________________________

Events in the story: ______________________________

____

____

____

____

____

____

____

____

____

E. Now write some ideas for imaginary stories using these themes.

"A Rescue Story" ______________________________

____

____

"A Prison Break" ______________________________

____

____

"A Story of Magic Powers" ______________________________

____

____

F. Choose one of your imaginary story topics and plan the details here. List in sequence all the events you would want to mention if you were to write the story.

Topic you chose: ______________________________

Events in the story: ______________________________

____

____

____

____

____

____

____

____

____

Write On

Look over the notes you wrote on a sequence of events for both the real story and the imaginary one. On another sheet of paper, write a story on the topic that appeals to you more. Add all of the interesting details you can think of, but keep the sequence clear.

Most stories are told in sequence—that is, the events of the story are presented in the order in which they happened.

lesson 2

Outlining and writing a report

A. You come home from school and notice this letter, addressed to you, lying on the hall table. (Please fill in the blanks.)

Dear ________________________,

We need someone of your age and superior intelligence to help us out on a dangerous mission to faraway ________________________. If you succeed, you will be famous at home and abroad.

Here are your instructions. Equip yourself as necessary and proceed directly to the city of ________________________. Your lodgings at the ________________________ Hotel have already been paid for. Use the name of ________________________ ________________________.

On ________________________ Mountain, which overlooks the city, lives ________________________, who appears ________________________ but is really ________________________. This person has ________________________, which we want because ________________________.

Upon your return, write us a complete report telling about your mission. Leave out no details, as everything is of interest to us. If we find your information to be accurate, you will be richly rewarded. Good luck.

Sincerely,

____

Your mission is a success. Now all that is left is to write the report. To make sure that you don't leave out anything important, you decide to organize your experiences in an **outline.** First, you write your ideas for the important general topics, or the **main heads** of the outline.

Travel to faraway ______________	Escape from ______________
Preparation for trip	Accomplishing my mission

Next, you sequence these topics. Since they tell a story, you decide to put them in a time sequence.

B. Write the main heads on the lines below in the order in which they happened. Each main head goes after a **Roman numeral.**

I. ______________________	III. ______________________
II. ______________________	IV. ______________________

Next, you start to fill in your outline with the details you'll want to include in your report. These are the subheads. The subheads you think of for "Preparation for trip" are:

Bought new clothes   Left notes for people   Bought necessary equipment

C. Arrange the subheads above on the outline below in the order that seems best to you. Each subhead goes after a **capital letter.**

I. Preparation for trip

A. ______________________________

1. ______________________________

2. ______________________________

B. ______________________________

1. ______________________________

2. ______________________________

C. ______________________________

1. ______________________________

2. ______________________________

D. Now you are ready to fill in the details below under each subhead. Write them after the **numbers** where they belong.

Cape   Teachers   Skis   Gloves   Parents   Ropes

E. Complete the phrases on the next page with details you make up. (Consult your letter to find out *where* you went, *whom* you saw, and *what* you went for.) Then continue your outline, adding the phrases under the proper topic headings.

First impressions of ________________

A problem getting away

How I got to see ________________

How my plan almost fails

Arrival at the hotel

Second part of the trip, from

________________ to ________________

Getting the ________________

II. Travel to faraway ________________

A. First part of trip, from ________________ to ________________

B. ____

III. Accomplishing my mission

A. ____

B. Going up the mountain

C. My first meeting with ________________

1. ____

2. ____

D. ____

1. My plan

2. ____

IV. Escape from ________________

A. ____

B. Solving the get-away problem

Here is one way you might use the information in the first part of your outline to write the report. Notice how the sentences in the paragraph *use* the information in the outline and *add to* it.

A. Bought new clothes
   1. Cape
   2. Gloves

First I went to the shopping center and bought myself a beautiful black wool cape lined with red satin. It had a hood and was warm enough, but I knew that my hands might get cold, so I found some black leather gloves on sale. The cape would take care of my making a distinguished appearance, and the gloves might come in handy in case I didn't want to leave any fingerprints.

F. Choose another subhead of the outline, circle it, and write it as a paragraph. The more details you give, the more interesting you make your writing.

____

____

____

____

____

____

Now design yourself some official-looking paper and write the report. Follow the sequence of the outline, but write your ideas as sentences. The topics and subtopics of the outline can also help you decide where to make paragraphs. Make your report as interesting and lively as you can by adding more details.

Use an outline to organize your ideas and put them in sequence before you write a report. Organize your outline into main heads, subheads, and details. When you write up your report, add more details to make the report more interesting.

lesson

3 Writing with flashbacks

Usually a story is told in sequence. Each event in the story takes place in order, one after the other. But sometimes a writer will use a **flashback.** A flashback interrupts the sequence of a story to show a scene or scenes that happened at an earlier time. In many flashback stories, the action begins in the present. Then the writer "flashes back" to show how things got to be the way they are. Read the following story.

> If you had told me at the beginning of the summer that by the end of it I'd be sitting here on the beach, five hundred miles away from my family, not sure of how I was going to get back home or even if I wanted to, I wouldn't have believed you. But then I hadn't counted on meeting Milton Turkle and that crazy pilot friend of his. And I hadn't counted on having Cousin Edward decide Milt could come live with us either. But I'm getting ahead of myself. Let me tell you how it all started.
>
> Last June, a few days after school let out, I was heading down toward the stream to get in some fishing. I wasn't thinking about much, except maybe supper, when I heard someone walking up behind me on the gravel path. "Looks like a good day for fishing," said this friendly voice, and I turned around and looked up at this fellow who must have been about six and a half feet tall. He was sort of half boy, half giant—tall and broad shouldered, but gangly. His teeth stuck out a little, and he grinned down at me and said, "Hi. Name's Milt Turkle here. How about you?"

A. Draw a line under the first sentence of the flashback in the story above.

B. Think of some ideas for a flashback story you could start. Look at the list of characters below and think of a present-time situation you could put each of them in that might require an explanation. Then think of a time to which each one might "flash back" to start his or her story.

A millionaire—At present: ______________________

Flashback: ______________________

A retired person—At present: ______________________

Flashback: ______________________

A child star—At present: ______________________

Flashback: ______________________

C. Pick the situation above that appeals to you most and start a flashback story. Write the story in the first person, as if you were the character. Tell something about where you are now. Then use a flashback to tell about an earlier time in your life when things were quite different for you.

____

____

____

____

____

____

____

____

____

____

____

____

____

____

Sometimes a writer uses a flashback to show you what is going on in a character's mind.

"Sissy Stobble, get in here!" yelled Sissy's mother Lettie from the doorway. She looked around the yard impatiently, sighed, and went inside, letting the screen door bang shut. Slam! Lettie Stobble winced, went over to turn off the stove, and then, for some reason, found she was thinking of her grandfather. That's right—the gate to his yard used to bang too. And that sound would alert him that she was coming in, even when he was dozing off on the porch swing.

"Eh? Now who's that coming in here making all that racket?" he'd say, in mock annoyance. "Why, if it isn't Lettie!" And he'd let her crawl up in his lap, and they'd swing back and forth and talk. Sometimes she'd even stay there past her own suppertime, and then her mother would be angry.

Slam! "Hi, Mom!" said Sissy, banging the door.

Lettie, startled, turned to look at her daughter. Sissy was all out of breath. Lettie smiled. "Hi, honey. Where have you been? Let me warm up your supper."

When something in the present reminds a person of something in the past, we say that it **triggers** a flashback.

D. Use the passage above to answer the questions below.

1. What triggered Lettie's flashback of her grandfather?

____

2. How did Lettie's flashback affect her attitude toward her daughter?

____

E. Below are six characters. Pick one and start a story. Tell a bit about that person and then "trigger" a flashback. The trigger you use should be something in the present that reminds the person of something in the past that was important to him or her in some way. The trigger might be the smell of some food, the sound of a song, the look of a person passing on the street, or something else.

an elderly person who is lonely
a child who is angry for being punished
a student who is daydreaming
someone in love
a person returning to his or her old school
an athlete who has just lost

Write On

Continue writing one of the flashback stories you started in part **C** or part **E**. Try to get inside the minds of your characters and to think the way they think.

A flashback interrupts the sequence of a story to tell of one or more events that happened at an earlier time. A flashback can show how a situation came to be the way it is, or it can tell what is happening in a character's mind.

lesson

Revising

Adding adverbs

Adverbs tell *how*, *when*, or *where* something happens. Some adverbs are single words, and some are **phrases**, or groups of words.

	How	**When**	**Where**
Adverbs	quickly quietly	now then	here there
Adverbial Phrases	with care with love	in an hour at noon	in the laundromat over the river

A. Write a sentence using each of the adverbs or adverbial phrases below.

1. (fortunately) ______________________________

2. (around the corner) ______________________________

3. (into the stew) ______________________________

4. (tomorrow) ______________________________

5. (immediately) ______________________________

Sentences can contain more than one adverb.

At midnight, a shadowy form slipped slowly over the balcony.

The position of an adverb in a sentence can sometimes be changed without changing the meaning of a sentence.

A shadowy form slowly slipped over the balcony at midnight.

B. Rewrite each sentence that follows. Add adverbs that answer the questions in parentheses.

1. The car rolled. (How? Where?)

____

2. We went out for pizza. (When? Where?)

____

3. The earth shook. (How? When? Where?)

____

Adverbs give you more specific information about what is happening. Compare these two paragraphs.

My sister Ida went walking. She realized a dog was trotting. When she patted him, he wagged his tail. She looked to find some sort of identification. When she started walking, the dog tagged along. And that is how we got Tags.

One drizzly afternoon, my sister Ida went walking down Main Street. After a few minutes she realized a dog was trotting alongside her. When she patted him on the head, he wagged his tail happily. She looked in vain to find some sort of identification. When she started walking back home, the dog tagged along beside her all the way. And that is how we got Tags.

C. Underline the adverbs in the second paragraph above. What kinds of information do they give you? ____

D. Now rewrite the paragraph below, adding adverbs where you think they would improve the story. Add your own ending.

There lived a witch. She waited, but no children wandered by. She devised a plan. She hung cookies and candies. Two small children did come. She greeted them. She invited them to try some sweets. . . .

____

____

____

____

____

____

____

Look over the papers you have written for this unit and see which ones might be improved by adding adverbs. Look for passages that need information about how, when, and where. Revise the papers, adding some adverbs that answer these questions clearly.

Add adverbs to your writing to give specific information about how, when, and where.

Post-Test

1. Number the following sentences in a sequence that makes sense.

_____ "What is that animal?" he asked a native Australian.

_____ "We don't have *ca ga rus* in England," said the man.

_____ The Australian stared at the man and said, "*Ca ga rus.*"

_____ In the Australian's language that meant, "I don't understand you."

_____ An early English settler was amazed to see a strange animal hopping across the plains of Australia.

_____ The animals have been called kangaroos ever since.

2. The partially completed outline below is on bicycles. Complete the outline by writing the heads and subheads where they belong.

Gear and chain repair; Pleasure and Relaxation; Fixing flat tires; Purposes for Bicycles; 3-speed bicycles

I. ______________________________

A. Transportation

B. ______________________________

II. Bicycle Maintenance

A. ______________________________

1. 10-speed bicycles

2. ______________________________

B. ______________________________

3. Add adverbs or adverbials to answer the questions in parentheses.

a. The tightrope walker walked ______________________. (where)

b. The tightrope slipped ______________________. (how, when)

c. The crowd gasped ______________________. (how, where)

4. In the first of three paragraphs, tell in sequence what you did in school today. Use one of the day's events to "trigger" a flashback to your first day in school. The flashback will be in the second paragraph. Then continue and complete your account of the day in the third paragraph.

unit 2
Writing About Cause and Effect

Things to Remember When Writing About Cause and Effect

A **cause** tells why something happens. An **effect** is what happens.

Writing

- State the main idea of a paragraph in a topic sentence.
- Put the topic sentence at the beginning of a paragraph to make the readers curious about what the rest of the paragraph will say.
- Put the topic sentence at the end of a paragraph to wrap up what has been said before.
- Have the topic sentence describe an effect and have the other sentences explain the causes in a cause-and-effect paragraph.
- Use a series of causes and effects to lead to the solution to the problem in a story.

Revising

- Use coordinate and subordinate conjunctions and conjunctive adverbs to show cause-and-effect relationships and to combine short, choppy sentences.

lesson

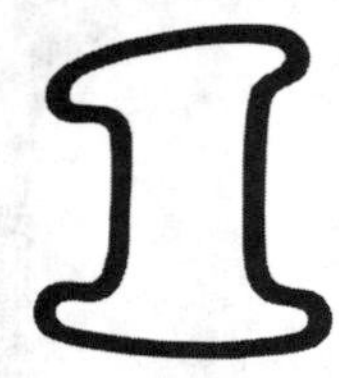

Topic sentences in cause-and-effect writing

Many paragraphs contain a **topic sentence,** a sentence that states the main idea of the whole paragraph. A topic sentence usually comes at the beginning or end of a paragraph.

A. Find the topic sentence for each paragraph that follows and underline it.

It was no accident that Nadine was the best tuba player in the county. Her parents had recognized her musical talent early and offered to pay for lessons on any instrument she chose. They were somewhat surprised when she picked the tuba, because it seemed a very large instrument for such a small girl. But Nadine loved the sound of it. She used to get up early so she could practice for an hour before breakfast. After school she would run home to build up her wind and then put in another two or three hours of practice. By the time she was old enough to carry her tuba around easily, she knew all the popular marches by heart.

First I pinned back my hair and covered my face with white greasepaint, smearing it up to my hairline and including my ears and neck. Next I took a black grease pencil and drew two upside-down V's above my natural eyebrows. I also drew black lines along my upper eyelids and extended them toward the sides of my face. With a red grease pencil I then made little round circles on my cheeks and painted my lips very full in the middle and thin toward the edges. All that was left was to put on my orange wig, baggy suit, and floppy shoes. And there I was, transformed into a clown, me and yet not me.

Both paragraphs describe cause-and-effect situations. A **cause** tells why something happens. An **effect** is what happens. One effect can have several causes.

B. Answer these questions about the paragraphs.

1. Do the topic sentences in the sample paragraphs describe causes or effects?

   ____

2. Do the sentences before and after the topic sentences describe causes or effects?

   ____

C. The topic sentences below all describe effects. If the sentence sounds like one that would begin a paragraph, put a *B* in front of it. If it sounds like one that would end a paragraph, put an *E* in front of it.

_______ 1. I knew from the first glance that there was going to be trouble.

_______ 2. That is why I cut my hair so short.

_______ 3. We've had to keep her locked up ever since.

_______ 4. I learned to roller skate the hard way.

_______ 5. As you see, it was only natural for me to become a lion tamer.

_______ 6. That's what I call a wasted day.

_______ 7. So you see, that's why I never get up before daylight.

_______ 8. Lee's strange behavior can be easily explained.

_______ 9. No one was surprised to hear that Joseph had gone to Alaska.

_______ 10. Flying is not difficult if you know the secret.

D. Pick one of the sentences in part **C.** Below, list three causes that could have produced that effect.

Sentence you chose: ______________________________

____

Causes: ______________________________

____

____

____

____

When a topic sentence comes at the beginning of a paragraph, it can make the readers curious about what the rest of the paragraph will go on to say.

When I came home, I was so angry I could hardly hang up my coat.

E. Fill in at least three blanks below with topic sentences that tell about specific times when you had strong feelings about something. Make your sentences as interesting as you can.

1. Happy: ______________________________

____

2. Sad: ______________________________

____

3. Amused: ______________________________

____

4. Angry: ______________________________

____

5. Surprised: ______________________________

____

6. Tired: ______________________________

____

F. Now choose one of the topic sentences above and use it to begin a paragraph. After you write the topic sentence, explain what caused you to feel that way.

When a topic sentence comes at the end of a paragraph, it can wrap up what has been said before.

For all of these reasons, I gave up playing marbles.

G. Write a topic sentence like the one above that gives a conclusion about some decision that you made.

H. Now write a paragraph using the topic sentence you just wrote at the end. The sentences before the last sentence should tell the reasons you had for making your decision.

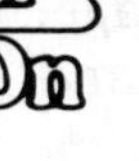

Turn back to part **C.** Pick another topic sentence and develop it into a paragraph, writing about the causes that led up to that effect.

A topic sentence gives the main idea of a paragraph. It usually comes at the beginning or end of a paragraph. In a cause-and-effect paragraph, if the topic sentence describes an effect, the other sentences should explain the causes.

lesson

2 Cause and effect in social studies and science

As I rounded the hedge, I could hear shouting coming from my porch. I saw my mother, my brother Luis, and the mail carrier all waving their hands and trying to talk at once. Our dog was yapping too, and Mother was trying to hold her. On the steps was a shattered package. Broken glass covered the steps.

The mail carrier was very excited. "I can't be responsible for this damage, Missus. I got bitten just last week. Four stitches. I was coming up the stairs and heard your dog . . ."

"I'm not blaming you," Mother interrupted. "I don't know why my son didn't do as he was told and keep the dog inside." She glared at Luis. "Couldn't you hear her jumping against the screen door, or was the TV too loud?"

Luis was red in the face. "That's my new aquarium that's busted all over the steps. Yes, I did hear the dog barking and jumping against the screen, but I thought you'd latched the door, Mom."

"I was in a hurry to get to work," said Mother, "and the door probably didn't catch. Now I'm really late."

"But what about my aquarium?" blubbered Luis.

The mail carrier broke in. "I couldn't see over the top of that package. I felt a dog around my legs. I was afraid that I'd go backward down the stairs."

They all started talking again. I stepped over the broken package, put my finger under the dog's collar, and took her inside. What a mess!

When we speak of cause and effect, we suggest that one action causes another. In many stories, it is not easy to identify the single cause of a situation. More often, several causes have led to the final event.

A. On the lines below, briefly describe the accident. Then list something that each character did to contribute to the accident.

The accident (effect): ______________________________

____

The causes: ______________________________

____

____

____

When we study a historical event, we are usually interested in the causes that led up to it. Here is an example.

Event: Columbus discovers the New World.
Causes: Columbus wishes to prove that the world is round.
Spain desires to open new trade routes to the East.
Queen Isabella gives Columbus money for the voyage.

B. Choose two of the historical events below. List two causes that led up to each.

the Gold Rush of '49
abolition of slavery in U.S.
American Revolution
U.S. women get right to vote
men land on moon
World War II

1. Event (effect): ______________________________

Causes: ______________________________

____

____

2. Event (effect): ______________________________

Causes: ______________________________

____

____

Scientists also study cause and effect. Many discoveries are made by observing how one action causes another. For example:

When a jar containing a burning candle is covered, the flame goes out.
(cause) (effect)

Sometimes, scientific discoveries or inventions are caused by a need for progress. For example:

People first made tools because they needed to cut up animals for food.
(effect) (cause)

Here are some other scientific discoveries and inventions.

the gas-powered engine
germs as causes of disease
the telephone
the telescope
the lever
the atom
anesthesia
electricity

C. Choose two of the discoveries or inventions above. For each, write a paragraph describing how life must have been without that knowledge. Then describe the effect of the discovery on our lives.

1. Discovery or invention: ______________________________

____

____

____

____

2. Discovery or invention: ______________________________

____

____

____

____

By careful observation, scientists can often predict the effect of a cause. For example:

If a scientist observes that water freezes below 0°C., he or she can predict that
(cause)
water placed in a freezer will turn into ice.
(effect)

D. What predictions can you make from the following information?

1. Observation: Thunder and lightning are seen in a darkening sky.

   Prediction: ____

   ____

2. Observation: Sunset is arriving at a later time each day.

   Prediction: ____

   ____

3. Observation: No oxygen is found in the atmosphere of planet X.

   Prediction: ____

   ____

4. Observation: As more land in Africa is cultivated, the food supply of many wild animals is eliminated.

   Prediction: ____

   ____

5. Observation: Factories are dumping wastes into rivers.

   Prediction: ____

   ____

Pick one of the social studies events you outlined earlier. Write a report on the event. You may wish to do a bit of research into its causes. You might also wish to discuss the effects the event has had on the world today.

In social studies and scientific writing, it is often important to show the causes and effects of an event.

lesson

3 Writing a story conflict and resolution

Tired from a day's work, you come home and pick up a book or turn on the TV. And what do you find?

1. Creatures from another galaxy are trying to take over the earth.

____

2. A sick young girl seems to be losing her will to live.

____

3. A crazy prowler is terrorizing a suburban neighborhood.

____

4. A prizefighter is trying to regain both his title and his dignity from his brash young opponent.

____

5. Victims of a shipwreck are struggling to survive on the high seas.

____

Each plot above involves a **conflict,** a struggle or confrontation of some kind. One of the satisfactions we get from reading stories and watching them on TV, in the movies, or in the theater, is seeing the successful ending, or **resolution,** to conflicts such as those above.

A. Think of a "happy ending" for each of the plots above. Write it on the line beneath the description of the conflict.

B. In stories, as in life, there are many kinds of conflict. Match each kind of conflict listed below with one of the story plots from the previous page. (Put the number of each plot on the lines here.)

______ 1. Between a person or people and nature

______ 2. Between groups

______ 3. Between an individual and a group

______ 4. Between two people

______ 5. Within one person

C. Think of at least three more story plots, each based on a different kind of conflict. After the appropriate conflicts below, write your three ideas in one or two sentences each.

1. Between a person or people and nature: ______________________

____

2. Between groups: ______________________

____

3. Between an individual and a group: ______________________

____

4. Between two people: ______________________

____

5. Within one person: ______________________

____

D. From the list of plots you made above, choose one you would like to develop into a story.

Which plot did you choose? ______________________

____

What is the conflict in this plot? ______________________

____

How will the conflict be resolved? ______________________

____

Now that you have the main ideas, you are ready to think of the events you will want to have in your story. Often, one event causes something to happen, which in turn causes something else to happen, and so forth. You can think of a story constructed in this way as a cause-and-effect **chain of events.**

For example, the chain of events leading up to the happy ending in Cinderella might look like this:

1. Cinderella's mother dies.
2. Cinderella's father remarries.
3. Cinderella's father dies.
4. Cinderella's stepmother's cruel nature emerges. She treats her own daughters well and makes Cinderella do all the work.
5. A ball at the palace is announced.
6. Cinderella's stepsisters go, but Cinderella doesn't.
7. Cinderella is unhappy.
8. Cinderella's Fairy Godmother appears and magically provides Cinderella with a coach, horses, and a gown. Now Cinderella can go to the ball.
9. At the ball, the Prince falls in love with Cinderella.
10. Cinderella flees at midnight when the Fairy Godmother's spell will be broken. Luckily she leaves a glass slipper behind.
11. The Prince searches for the woman whose foot will fit the glass slipper.
12. The Prince finds Cinderella; they marry and live happily ever after.

E. Some of the events in the story had to happen before other events could take place. Draw an arrow from each event that seems to have caused or made possible the event which follows. The first one has been done for you.

F. List the chain of events you will use for your story. Think about what events will cause the conflict. Then think of what events will cause the resolution.

Write On

Now you are ready to write your story of conflict and resolution. Use the chain of events as an outline and add details and dialogue to make the story come alive.

Many short stories contain a conflict and resolution. A series of causes and effects often leads to the solution.

Revising

Combining sentences with cause-and-effect words

Throughout this unit, you have learned about cause and effect. Certain words in our language show how thoughts or actions are related. These words are called **coordinate conjunctions, subordinate conjunctions,** and **conjunctive adverbs.** Here are some examples.

Coordinate Conjunctions		Subordinate Conjunctions		Conjunctive Adverbs	
and	nor	when	because	consequently	thus
but	yet	since	if	therefore	rather
or	for	so	although	nevertheless	instead
		unless	before	however	still
		after	while		
		until	as		

Conjunctions and conjunctive adverbs are particularly helpful in showing cause and effect. Notice the difference between the sentences below.

The gun fired. The cat jumped.
When the gun fired, the cat jumped.

A. Combine each pair of sentences below. Use a conjunction or conjunctive adverb to show a cause-and-effect relationship.

1. I would love to go on the camping trip. I hurt my leg.

____

2. Give me that notebook. I paid for it.

____

3. I must clean my room. I can go to the movies.

____

4. Yoko came to visit me. I stopped doing my homework.

____

5. I was hot and tired. I drank a glass of iced tea.

____

6. Teresa's painting was the best. It won first prize.

____

7. Walter was bored. He drummed his fingers on the table.

____

B. The paragraph below has short, choppy sentences, and it is confusing. Revise the paragraph so that the reader will understand clearly the causes and effects of the fire. You may rearrange the order of the sentences.

There was a fire in the hospital. The fire happened early one morning. No one knows how it happened. There were not many people around early that morning. There was very little smoke. Not many people saw any smoke. The nurses did not smell anything. The doctors did not smell anything. The fire started on the first floor. The fire spread quickly to the upper floors. The fire alarm on the first floor did not work. A lot of damage was done there. The fire engines finally arrived. The fire was soon put out.

Write On

Look back at the "Write On" exercises you have written for this unit. Have you clearly shown cause-and-effect relationships? Choose one "Write On" and underline all the conjunctions and conjunctive adverbs you have used. Find any short, choppy, or unclear sentences. Rewrite the paragraph, adding conjunctions and conjunctive adverbs.

Use coordinate and subordinate conjunctions and conjunctive adverbs to show cause-and-effect relationships and to combine short, choppy sentences.

Post-Test

1. After reading the paragraph, underline its topic sentence.

As soon as we bought the house, we cleared the rubbish out of the yards. Then we planted a lawn and trees. During the summer we repaired the porches and had a new roof put on. It took all our spare time this fall to paint the outside of the house. We really worked hard to make the house look great.

2. Does the topic sentence in the paragraph above describe a cause or an effect?

____

3. Match each cause in history and science with its effect. Write the letter of the effect in the blank next to its cause.

______ There is no rain all summer.	a. America declares war.
______ The moon passes between the earth and the sun.	b. Many crops die.
______ Japanese war planes bomb Pearl Harbor, Hawaii.	c. American soldiers are poorly fed and supplied.
______ The Continental Army has no money.	d. The day grows dark.

4. Combine each pair of sentences below. Use a conjunction or a conjunctive adverb to show the cause-and-effect relationship between the sentences.

a. Our balloon has a rip in it. We must walk across the jungle.

____

b. We can't buy an elephant. Our rhinos take up too much room at home.

____

c. The shop was giving away ice cream. Children lined up for two blocks.

____

5. Write a *C* next to each conflict. Write *R* next to each resolution.

______ When the circus lions escaped, everyone in town was afraid.

______ Now even Mom agreed it was fun to have a horse.

______ Year after year, Mom told Jan it would be impossible to own a horse.

______ With the lions in their cages, everyone could enjoy the circus.

6. Use one of the above conflicts and the corresponding resolution in a story. Write a cause-and-effect chain of events to tell how the conflict was resolved.

unit 3
Writing Details

Things to Remember About Writing with Details

Details are small bits of information.

Writing

- Use sense details in descriptions.
- Emphasize certain details, depending on the point of view you are using or the point you want to make.
- Include details about physical appearance and personality when describing a character.
- Use a description of the place, weather, and time in a story to create a mood or give information about your characters.

Revising

- Add modifiers to make your writing clear and specific.
- Avoid unnecessary modifiers.
- Correct misplaced or dangling modifiers.

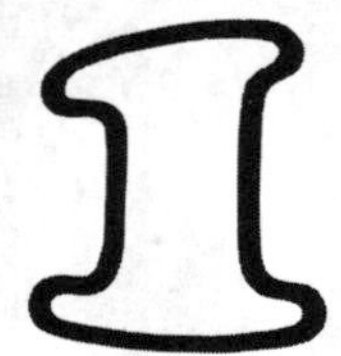

lesson

Choosing details for writing

Look at the picture on this page. Of course, you see many things. We often depend on our sense of sight to enjoy and describe the world around us. But our other senses are just as important; we can often get as much information from them as we can from our sense of sight.

A. Put yourself into the picture on this page, and answer the questions that follow.

1. What sounds might you hear? Just list details; you don't need complete sentences.

_______________ _______________

_______________ _______________

2. What things would you expect to smell?

3. What might you taste if you were there?

4. What could you touch or feel?

B. Think about a completely different place, such as a city or a desert. Write a topic sentence that gives your general impression of the place. Then complete the paragraph with sense details. Try to use at least two details for each sense.

The picture above shows the Screech Owls giving a concert. They are singing their new hit, "Screaming Mimi." Think about how they look and how they might sound.

C. In the spaces below, list as many details as you can about the Screech Owls.

Appearance: ____

____

____

____

____

Instruments and sounds: ____

____

____

____

____

You can list many details about the rock group. But you can choose to emphasize only certain details, depending on the point you want to make.

D. Pretend you are a Screech Owls fan. What details about the concert will you list in your diary?

____

____

____

____

E. Pretend you live next door to the concert hall. What details will you mention when you call the police to complain?

____

____

____

____

F. Pretend you are a music critic. What details will you include in notes for your review?

____

____

____

____

Write On Choose one of the following places. On another paper, list as many sense details as you can about it. Then write two descriptions of the place—one from each point of view listed next to the place.

your favorite restaurant—to you and to a waiter or waitress
a courtroom—to a judge and to a defendant
a hospital room—to a patient and to a nurse

Sense details add to descriptions. Writers may choose to emphasize certain details, depending on their point of view or the point they want to make.

lesson

Describing a character

Every person you meet is unique. Nobody looks or acts exactly like anyone else. One of the challenges of describing a person in writing is seeing if you can pin down in words just what it is about that person that gives you a sense of him or her.

Read this description of Mr. Bounderby from Charles Dickens's *Hard Times* and look for the details that describe the man's appearance and character.

> He was a rich man: banker, merchant, manufacturer, and what not. A big, loud man, with a stare, and a metallic laugh. A man made of coarse material, which seemed to have been stretched to make so much of him. A man with a great puffed head and forehead, swelled veins in his temples, and such a strained skin to his face that it seemed to hold his eyes open and lift his eyebrows up. A man with a pervading appearance on him of being inflated like a balloon, and ready to start. . . . He had not much hair. One might have fancied he had talked it off, and that what was left, all standing up in disorder, was in that condition from being constantly blown about by his windy boastfulness.

A. Reread the description of Mr. Bounderby and fill in the lines below with the details asked for.

1. Profession and condition in life: ______________________

____

2. Size and general impression: ______________________

____

3. Comparison (What did it seem he was made of?): ______________________

____

4. Head: ______________________

____

5. Seeming function of skin on face: ______________________

____

6. Comparison that gives overall impression: ______________________

____

7. Condition of hair and reason for it: ______________________________

____

B. Make a list below of some details you could use in describing a character. Pick someone you know fairly well, or invent someone who is the opposite of Mr. Bounderby in every respect you can imagine.

1. Name, occupation, and condition in life: ______________________

____

2. Size and overall physical impression: ________________________

____

3. Specific physical details (anything particularly noticeable about eyes, hair, expressions, nose, mouth, ears, skin, or body): ______________

____

____

____

____

____

____

4. Disposition (grumpy, lively, and so on): ______________________

____

5. Comparisons (Does this person or anything about this person remind you of anyone or anything?): ______________________________

____

6. Typical ways of moving: ________________________________

____

7. Typical way of dressing: ________________________________

____

Mr. Bounderby and the person you wrote about in part **B** were both described in a fairly realistic way. But characters in comic strips, adventure stories, and fantasies often have some superhuman powers or other unrealistic traits. Read this description of Mabel the Mighty and think about how she is special.

> Strong and powerful, Mabel the Mighty could swing through the trees with speed and grace. Her arms seemed longer than usual for a young woman, and no doubt they were, since Mabel had known no other parents than chimpanzees. Chimpanzees had rescued her on the equator, where she had been mysteriously abandoned as a baby; naturally, she had imitated them in everything. Whenever she needed to rest, she would squat on a branch, her long dry fingers playing idly with her matted hair. Exposure to the wind, rain, and sun had made her skin tough and leathery, but she still needed the leopard skin she wore loosely-draped over her strong shoulders to protect her from the wind. She often wondered why she didn't have a thick furry coat like her brothers and sisters.

C. Now invent your own story or comic-strip character who is superstrong or superclever, or who has some other super power. Your character can be human, partly human, or nonhuman. The more details you can think of to describe your character, the more real and interesting he, she, or it will become. List the details here.

1. Name of character: ______________________

2. Nature of character (What kind of being is it?): ______________________

____

3. Super characteristic of the character: ______________________

____

4. Size and overall physical impression: ______________________

____

5. Specific physical details (eyes, nose, mouth, skin, body, and so on): ______

____

____

____

____

6. Disposition (evil, friendly, and so on): ______________________

____

7. Comparisons (Does your character or part of your character look like anyone or anything?): ______________________________

____

8. Other details of personality or appearance: ______________________________

____

D. In parts **B** and **C** you listed details to describe two different characters. Now write a descriptive paragraph about one of them. You may want to start or end your paragraph with a topic sentence that gives a general impression of the character.

____

____

____

____

____

____

____

____

Write On

Write a story about the character you described in part **D,** using your description as the first paragraph. Or if you wish, you may write a paragraph describing the other character about whom you listed details.

A description of a character can include details about physical appearance and personality.

lesson

Describing a setting

A story includes characters and a plot. The bare facts of a story may be quite simple. Read this story beginning.

> One day Scrooge was busy in his countinghouse while his clerk was copying letters in another room.

Do you learn much about Scrooge, his clerk, or the day?

Another important story element is the **setting.** The setting—a description of the place, the weather, the time—often helps to create a mood or give information about the characters. Read the passage about Scrooge as Charles Dickens wrote it.

> Once upon a time—of all the good days in the year, upon a Christmas Eve—old Scrooge sat busy in his countinghouse. It was cold, bleak, biting, foggy weather; and the city clocks had only just gone three, but it was quite dark already.
>
> The door of Scrooge's countinghouse was open, that he might keep his eye upon his clerk, who, in a dismal little cell beyond, a sort of tank, was copying letters. Scrooge had a very small fire, but the clerk's fire was so very much smaller that it looked like one coal.

A. Explain what the description of the setting above adds to the bare facts. What details do you learn about the day and about Scrooge and the clerk?

____

____

____

____

____

Characters and settings can interact. The way a character reacts to a setting can tell a lot about the character. Meet Millicent McGurk (pictured at the top of page 43), a character in search of a setting.

B. Think about Millicent. What does she look like? What kind of a person do you think she is? Write a few details about Millicent on the lines below.

Appearance: ____

____

Character traits: ____

____

C. Below are pictures of two settings. Put Millicent into each one. Think about how she would react to the physical place, as well as to any animals or people there. Then write a story beginning that describes Millicent in each setting.

Setting 1: ____

____

____

____

____

Setting 2: ____

____

____

____

____

In some kinds of stories, the setting plays an especially important role. Mystery writers, for example, often get their ideas by just the kind of observation you have been doing in this unit: thinking about how things look, smell, sound, and so on. When you know just how a thing ought to be, any little change can suggest a mystery. Read this short passage.

> The boat was moored in its usual spot. The sails were neatly furled, and the brass shone in the moonlight. Everything looked natural to Cal, but something was disturbing him. "I can't quite put my finger on what's wrong," he sniffed to himself. Then he sniffed again. What was that strange, sweet smell—like dead roses?

D. Use the passage above to do these activities.

1. List three details about the setting.

___

___

___

2. Which detail makes the setting mysterious?

___

E. Now you try writing a description of a mystery setting. Choose one of the places below to describe. Then add one or two details that are out of place.

your house or room	a museum
a carnival	a toy store

___

___

___

___

___

___

___

___

___

___

___

Science fiction stories usually take place in another world or another time. The setting and plot are often closely related. A story set on a special planet, star, or world must take into account the way that place works and special problems such a place may have.

F. Create your own science fiction setting. You may wish to use one of the details below as part of your setting.

water instead of air
everything made of unbreakable plastic
no sun for light or warmth
plants that eat humans

Now write a description of your setting. If you wish, put yourself or another character in it.

____

____

____

____

____

____

____

____

____

Choose one of the settings you described for part **C**, part **E**, or part **F** to use as the beginning of a short story. Add any characters you wish, and create a plot. Write your story on another sheet of paper.

The setting is a description of a place and time. In many stories, especially mystery and science fiction stories, a description of the place and time is important to the characters and plot.

Revising

lesson

Using modifiers

Adjectives, adverbs, prepositional phrases, participles, clauses—all these words and word groups are **modifiers.** Modifiers help make sentences specific, clear, and colorful. However, too many modifiers can overload your sentences. Look at these examples.

Overloaded: The hungry, starving cat that hadn't eaten for days gulped the cream quickly.

Better: The starving cat hungrily gulped the cream.

A. Revise each overloaded sentence below. Choose enough modifiers to make the sentence clear and specific. Strengthen nouns and verbs if you wish.

1. The frightened, terrified child, who seemed to be lost, alone, and by himself, screamed loudly with a loud shriek for his mother.

____

____

2. Beautiful, colorful, lovely flowers, including tulips and daffodils, filled the garden with color, loveliness, and perfume.

____

____

3. A large, enormous, sparkling diamond lay glowing in the center of the soft, smooth, velvet-lined case that was lined with maroon-colored velvet.

____

____

4. Struggling under the heavy weight, a small, tiny, little girl carried a big, huge, heavy box that was wrapped in bright, gay, colorful paper.

____

____

Modifiers should be placed as close as possible to the words they modify. Otherwise, they are called **misplaced modifiers.** If there is no word in the sentence that a modifier can sensibly modify, we say the modifier **dangles.** In that case, you must add such a word to the sentence. Look at these examples.

Misplaced: Pablo caught three trout wearing new wading boots.
Revised: Wearing new wading boots, Pablo caught three trout.

Dangling: In her new disco skates, the evening was great fun.
Revised: In her new disco skates, Julie enjoyed the evening.

B. Revise each sentence below to correct the misplaced or dangling modifier.

1. As a known dealer in stolen goods, the police were always after Alonzo.

2. Having a hungry family of eight puppies, one can of dog food a day wasn't enough.

3. Reading a scary mystery, the howling dog disturbed Marjorie.

4. The vet came to see the cow in the barn that was mooing loudly.

5. Greg gave a valentine to Cindy with a red heart and white lace.

Look over the papers you have written for this unit. Check to see that you have used modifiers to make your sentences clear and specific but have not overloaded any sentence. Also look for misplaced or dangling modifiers to correct. Choose one paper and revise it.

Use modifiers to make your writing clear and specific, but don't overuse them. Check your writing to be sure you have no misplaced or dangling modifiers.

Post-Test

1. Finish the following sentence to describe the character in two ways.

Fifteen-year-old Jason Linn was a boy who . . .

a. Give four realistic details about Jason's appearance.

b. Give three nonrealistic details about Jason's unusual powers.

2. Read the description of this setting.

The school was a modern low brick building surrounded by wide, grassy lawns. A playground and baseball diamond were behind the school.

a. Add one detail to make the scene above into a science fiction setting.

b. Add one detail to make the scene above into a mystery setting.

3. Revise each sentence to correct overloaded or misplaced modifiers.

a. Under the bed, squashed and dusty, Claire found her good hat.

b. With a loud noise, the great, huge, tall giant crashed loudly and noisily into Mother's beautiful, lovely, antique china.

c. Flying at an altitude of 2000 feet, the lake looked tiny.

4. Write three paragraphs about a person you know and the setting where you see him or her most frequently. In the first paragraph, give a complete physical description of the person. In the second paragraph, tell about the person's personality, occupation or activities, and general condition in life. In the third paragraph, describe the setting where you often see the person.

unit 4
Writing Comparisons

Things to Remember About Writing Comparisons

Comparisons show likenesses. **Contrasts** show differences.

Writing

- Compare two items in a paragraph by starting the paragraph with a topic sentence and ending it with a concluding sentence.
- Use comparative words and expressions such as *easier, more expensive than,* and *less than* to help you make comparisons.
- Use similes, metaphors, and personification to make your comparisons more interesting. Remember that similes compare two things by using *like* or *as.* Metaphors say one thing is another thing. Personification suggests that an inanimate thing is alive.
- Make your character descriptions clearer and more lively by comparing and contrasting the characters.

Revising

- Replace general adjectives with specific, concrete sense adjectives to make your descriptions vivid.

lesson

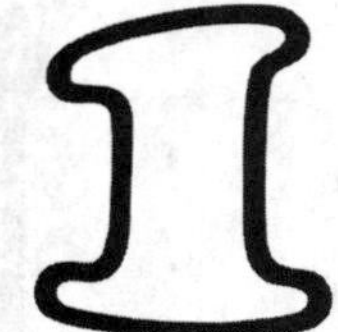

Writing a paragraph with comparisons

In the picture on this page, people are gathering for a journey around the world. Each traveler has chosen a different means of transportation.

A. Look at the picture again.

1. Which vehicle would be the fastest? ______________________

2. Which vehicle would be the slowest? ______________________

3. Which vehicle would be the most comfortable? ______________

4. Which vehicle would be the most interesting? _______________

B. If you had a chance to travel around the world, which method of transportation would you choose? On the lines below, give the reasons for your choice.

____

____

____

You were just comparing different methods of transportation. It often helps to compare things when you have decisions to make. When you buy something, for example, you want to choose the item that best suits your needs. Comparing the features of two or more items can help you make the decision more easily.

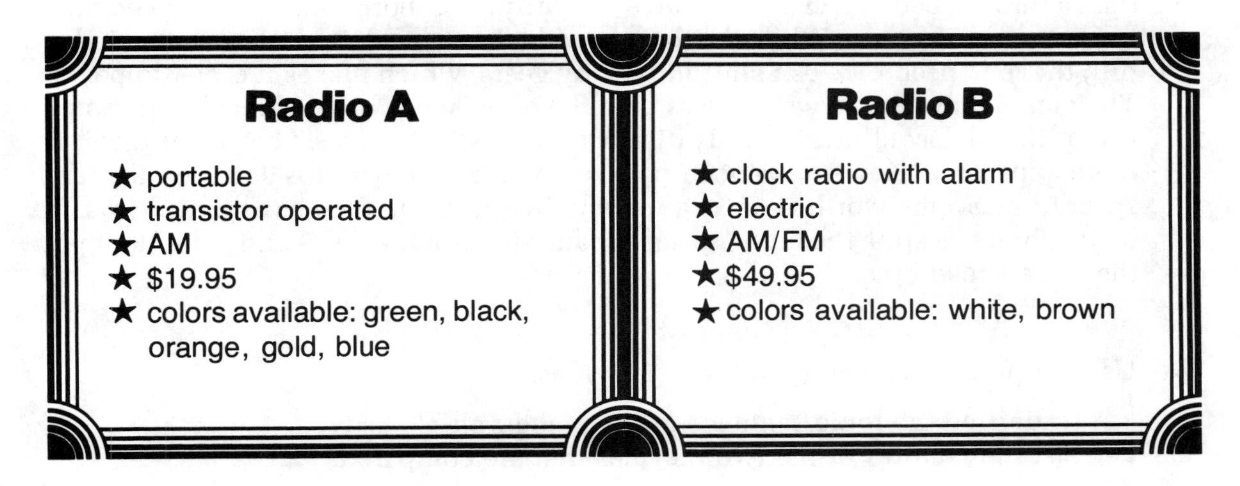

C. Looks at the two ads above. In the first column of the chart below, list four features you would want to compare before you buy one of the radios. Then complete the chart by listing how each radio compares. The first feature has been done for you.

	Feature	Radio A	Radio B
1.	portable	yes	no
2.			
3.			
4.			

When comparing two items, we often use **comparative forms** of adjectives and adverbs. For example, if you are comparing the price of Radio A and Radio B, you could say:

Radio B is more expensive than Radio A.
Radio A is less expensive than Radio B.

OR

The price of Radio B is higher than that of Radio A.
The price of Radio A is lower than that of Radio B.

OR

Radio A costs less than Radio B.
Radio B costs more than Radio A.

If you are in doubt about how to use comparative forms, consult page 118 in the Handbook.

Here is an example of a paragraph that compares two items. Notice the comparative forms that are used.

There are several reasons why I chose to buy a ten-speed racing bicycle rather than a three-speed bicycle. Since I live in a hilly neighborhood, the ten-speed bike has advantages for me. While the three-speed bike can use only one gear to climb a hill, the ten-speed bike can shift into many gears, which makes it easier to pedal. The racing bicycle also weighs less than the three-speed bike. Therefore, it can go up a hill with less effort. The only disadvantage of the ten-speed bicycle is that it is more expensive. However, since I plan to go on a bike trip this summer, the ten-speed bike seems worth the extra money. In short, the ten-speed bicycle was a better choice despite the higher price because it has more gears and is lighter than the three-speed bike.

D. Use the passage above to do these activities.

1. Underline the topic sentence of the paragraph.
2. List the features of the two bicycles that are compared.

____

____

3. List the comparative words or expressions that are used in the paragraph. The first one has been done for you.

easier ____________________ ____________________

____________________ ____________________

____________________ ____________________

____________________ ____________________

E. Now choose one of the following topic sentences for a paragraph you will write. Complete the sentence to reflect your preferences.

1. If I could choose, I would rather live in a ____________________ climate than a ____________________ one.
2. My choice of a perfect pet would be a ____________________ rather than a ____________________.
3. I would rather watch a TV program about ____________________ than about ____________________.
4. I would rather be ____________________ than ____________________.

F. After you have completed your topic sentence, fill in the grid below to help you compare the features you will include in your paragraph.

Features	Item A (________)	Item B (________)

G. You may wish to use the paragraph at the top of the previous page as a model for your paragraph. Begin with a topic sentence, and end with a statement that sums up your reasons for making your choice.

Write On

On a separate sheet of paper, write a paragraph explaining a choice or decision you have recently made or expect to make in the future. Remember to include a topic sentence and a concluding sentence. Use comparative words and expressions to help you compare and contrast.

A paragraph that compares two items should begin with a topic sentence and end with a concluding sentence. Comparative words and expressions help you make comparisons.

lesson

2 Writing metaphors and similes

All the world's a stage,
And all the men and women merely players:
They have their exits and their entrances;
And one man in his time plays many parts. . . .

— *William Shakespeare*

In the lines above, Shakespeare compares the world to a stage. A comparison in which a writer says that one thing is another thing is called a **metaphor.**

A. Look back at the quotation to see how the metaphor of the world's being a stage is continued.

1. What are men and women compared to? ______________________

2. What in life do you think entrances and exits refer to? ______________________

____

3. What parts, or roles, have you played in your life so far? ______________________

____

Life is like a school of gladiators, where men live and fight with one another.
—*Seneca*

Life is like a scrambled egg.
—*Don Marquis*

Life is as tedious as a twice-told tale. . . .
—*Shakespeare*

In the quotations you just read, the writers compared life to several different things. A comparison in which the writer compares one thing to another using the words *like* or *as* is called a **simile.**

B. Look back at the quotations once more and think about each of the comparisons.

1. Why do you think Seneca used the word *school* in his comparison? ______

____

2. In what ways is life like a scrambled egg? ______________________

____

3. In what ways is life like "a twice-told tale"? ____________________

____

C. Read the comparisons below. Put an *S* in front of each simile and an *M* in front of each metaphor.

______ 1. Friendship is a sheltering tree. (Samuel Taylor Coleridge)

______ 2. Like an army defeated/The snow hath retreated (William Wordsworth)

______ 3. Oh, my love is like a red, red rose (Robert Burns)

______ 4. I slept, and dreamed that life was Beauty;/I woke, and found that life was Duty. (Ellen Sturgis Hooper)

______ 5. Love is sunshine, hate is shadow,/Life is checkered shade and sunshine. (Henry Wadsworth Longfellow)

______ 6. Time is like a river. (Marcus Aurelius)

D. Choose one of the comparisons in part **C.** On the lines below, explain how you think the two things being compared are alike.

____

____

____

E. Write some metaphors and similes of your own. Complete each comparison below.

1. My bed is like ______________________________

2. The sun is ______________________________

3. Home is as ______________________________ as ______________________________.

4. Life is ______________________________

Sometimes, instead of calling one thing by another thing's name, a writer will make a statement that suggests than an inanimate (nonliving) thing is alive. Since the object is often given some characteristics of a person, we call this kind of writing **personification.** Look at the example below.

> I heard the trailing garments of the Night
> Sweep through her marble halls
>
> —*Henry Wadsworth Longfellow*

F. Use the quotation above to answer the questions below.

1. What is personified in the lines by Longfellow? ______________

2. In what way is this inanimate thing made to seem human? ______________

____

Now read this poem.

I Wandered Lonely as a Cloud

I wandered lonely as a cloud
That floats on high o'er vales and hills,
When all at once I saw a crowd,
A host, of golden daffodils;
Beside the lake, beneath the trees,
Fluttering and dancing in the breeze.

Continuous as the stars that shine
And twinkle on the milky way,
They stretched in never-ending line
Along the margin of a bay:
Ten thousand saw I at a glance,
Tossing their heads in sprightly dance.

The waves beside them danced; but they
Outdid the sparkling waves in glee:
A poet could not but be gay,
In such a jocund company:
I gazed—and gazed—but little thought
What wealth the show to me had brought:

For oft, when on my couch I lie,
In vacant or in pensive mood,
They flash upon that inward eye
Which is the bliss of solitude;
And then my heart with pleasure fills,
And dances with the daffodils.

—William Wordsworth

G. Refer to Wordworth's poem to answer the following.

1. Write two similes from the poem.

____

____

2. List the things in the poem that are personified as dancing.

____

3. How do you think the poet's mood changes, and why?

____

H. Think of a time when you were feeling especially good or bad. Write a metaphor or simile that expresses how you felt. You might say something like "I felt like a puppy sprawled out in the sun" or "I was a crumpled newspaper, tossed away and forgotten."

____

____

Choose one of the writing ideas below.

1. Write a poem about a mood of yours in which each line is a metaphor or simile that describes that mood. Each line should begin "I was ______" or "I felt like ______."
2. Write a poem or paragraph that tells of a time when you were in a particular mood and something you saw changed it, the way seeing the daffodils changed Wordsworth's mood in "I Wandered Lonely as a Cloud." Try to include similes, metaphors, and personification.

Comparisons can be made with similes, metaphors, and personification. Similes compare two things using like or as; metaphors say one thing is another thing; personification suggests inanimate things are alive.

lesson 3

Comparing characters

Jane was as thin as a snake. Her arms and legs were like twigs that seemed to be sprouting so that her clothes were never quite big enough. Her Uncle Sid said that she looked like Aunt Alice, but there was no way of telling for sure, since Alice had departed this earth some thirty years before Jane was born.

A. Use the description of Jane to answer the questions below.

1. What animal is Jane compared to? ______________________________
2. What object is she compared to? ______________________________
3. What other person is she compared to? ______________________________

Writers often make their descriptions of characters more vivid and interesting by using comparisons.

B. Does anyone you know remind you of a spatula or a bookmark? A rhinoceros or a chipmunk? Write down the names of ten people you know fairly well. After each one, write an object or animal that the person reminds you of. Do this as quickly as possible; jot down anything that comes to mind.

____

____

____

____

____

C. Choose two of the people from part **B** and write two or three sentences describing each person. Include your comparison and any details about the person's appearance or personality that are relevant to the comparison.

1.

2.

Iris asked Karen to go down to the baseball diamond after school and take a message to Boris. "You will recognize him easily," she said. "He's the tallest one on the team."

D. How would you describe the other members of the team pictured on page 59 in relation to each other. By comparing the physical appearance of each one with the others, tell Karen how she could recognize these team members.

Caesar: ______________________________

Eric: ______________________________

Hiram: ______________________________

Irving: ______________________________

Lem was as lazy as Juanita was energetic. As she bustled about, cleaning and repairing, he lay motionless in the hammock. Even when she sat down, Juanita was never completely still: Her toe would tap, her fingers would drum. Lem occasionally opened one eye and resettled his pipe in the other corner of his mouth.

E. In the paragraph above, two characters are being **contrasted**—that is, their differences are being pointed out. Use the paragraph to answer these questions.

1. What was Lem like? ______________________________

____

2. What was Juanita like? ______________________________

____

3. Which character—Lem or Juanita—probably does each of the following?

washes the car ____________

sleeps late every day ____________

bought a remote-control device for the TV ____________

takes tap dancing lessons ____________

F. Choose two characters who are opposite in some way. They may be people you know or characters you create. Here are some contrasts you may use.

big and small | kind and cruel
pleasant and grouchy | quick and slow

Fill in the topic sentence below with the contrasting features of your characters. Then write a paragraph that develops the contrast.

________________ (character) was as ________________ (feature) as

________________ (character) was ________________ (feature).

____

____

____

____

____

____

____

____

____

Write On

Think about your family and friends. Who are you most like—a parent, a brother, a great-aunt? In what ways—appearance, mannerisms, personality—are you similar to this person? In what ways are you different? On another sheet of paper, write two paragraphs. In the first, show how you are like a relative or friend. In the second, contrast yourself with that person.

One way to describe a character is to use comparison. You may point out how the character is like someone or something else, or you may contrast two characters—that is, point out the differences.

Revising

Choosing adjectives

Adjectives describe, define, or limit nouns. We use special forms of adjectives to compare two or more objects, animals, or people.

an expensive radio
a more expensive radio
the most expensive radio

a lazy man
a lazier man
the laziest man

There are a great many adjectives to choose from. Many adjectives can be formed by adding endings to nouns or verbs. Notice the endings used below.

grace—gracious
enjoy—enjoyable

create—creative
music—musical

storm—stormy
fret—fretful

A. Form an adjective from each word below by adding an appropriate ending. You may need to make spelling changes. Check your dictionary if you're not sure of the correct spelling.

1. exception ____________
2. consider ____________
3. continue ____________
4. fright ____________
5. impress ____________
6. mischief ____________
7. critic ____________
8. dust ____________

B. You can use your senses to discover adjectives. Think about how the following nouns look, feel, smell, sound, and/or taste. Fill in the lines below with sense adjectives to describe each noun. You may "borrow" from nouns and verbs to come up with adjectives.

1. the ocean ____________ ____________ ____________
2. a motorcycle ____________ ____________ ____________
3. chocolate fudge ____________ ____________ ____________
4. a supermarket ____________ ____________ ____________
5. a kitten ____________ ____________ ____________

The more specific you can be in your writing, the better. People often use adjectives like *nice* or *funny* or *good* to give a general impression of something or someone. However, if you are writing a description and your goal is to get across the particular flavor or character of the person or event you are describing, then you would do well either to avoid using such general adjectives or to explain them more fully.

Which sentence gives you a clearer impression of the person described?

She is a nice person, and she enjoys sharing good food.
The minute I came in the door, she took some hard garlicky sausage and nutted cheese out of the refrigerator and invited me to share them with her.

C. Rewrite the following descriptions, making them more specific. Invent details and use sense adjectives where appropriate.

1. He wore a funny costume.

____

____

2. The meal tasted awful.

____

____

3. We enjoyed the nice music.

____

____

4. His new shoes felt bad.

____

____

5. The house smelled strange.

____

____

Look over the papers you have written for this unit. Check for sentences that can use more specific adjectives and details. Choose one paper and revise it.

Use specific, concrete sense adjectives and details to make your descriptions vivid.

Post-Test

1. Use the grid below to compare two features of drying clothes with a clothesline or a dryer.

Features	**Clothesline**	**Dryer**
______________	______________	______________
______________	______________	______________

2. Write S in front of each simile below. Write *M* in front of each metaphor. Write *P* in front of each example of personification.

_____ a. I am as strong as a bull moose!—Theodore Roosevelt

_____ b. Love is the jewel that wins the world.—Moira O'Neill

_____ c. Time has fallen asleep in the afternoon sunshine.—Alexander Smith

_____ d. Time is only the stream I go fishing in.—Henry Thoreau

_____ e. A promise made is a debt unpaid.—William Service

_____ f. Because I could not stop for Death,/He kindly stopped for me;
The carriage held but just ourselves/and Immortality.
—Emily Dickinson

3. Rewrite the descriptions below. Invent details and use sense adjectives to make the sentences more specific.

a. The food tasted bad. ______________________________

____

b. The band's music sounds interesting. ______________________________

____

c. Our new teacher is good. ______________________________

____

4. Write a paragraph that compares your favorite TV character with a favorite character from a book. Name at least three ways in which the characters are alike and three ways in which they are different.

unit 5
Writing Facts and Opinions

Things to Remember About Writing Facts and Opinions

A **fact** is an objective statement that can be tested or checked. An **opinion** is a subjective statement that expresses someone's feelings or ideas.

Writing

- Use only facts in an objective article such as a news story. Express your feelings and opinions in a subjective article such as an editorial, a review, or a feature story.
- Use factual information in a research report. Begin the report with an introductory paragraph and present the facts in a logical order.
- Use plus-loaded words like *attractive* and *useful,* and minus-loaded words like *embarrassed* and *worried* when writing opinions.

Revising

- Replace vague words with specific nouns and verbs to make your sentences clear and accurate.

lesson 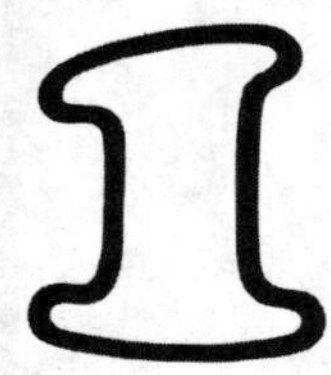

Writing objective and subjective articles

A visit to sunny Florida, the most beautiful state in the Union, is something you will never forget. Florida was discovered in 1513 by Ponce de León. This year, you too will discover paradise when you relax on Florida's magnificent beaches and fish along its vast coastline. A boat ride through the lush Everglades National Park will thrill you. The five-thousand-square-mile preserve contains a multitude of tropical plants and animals. You will love seeing Cape Canaveral. It is here that the world's first moon flight was launched in 1969. If you join the thousands who choose Florida, the Orange Blossom State, you will have the vacation of a lifetime.

The advertisement on page 66 has used both facts and opinions to try to persuade its readers. A **fact** is a statement that can be tested or checked to see if it is true. We call a fact an **objective** statement. An **opinion** expresses someone's feelings or ideas. It cannot be checked or tested. Opinions often contain verbs like *think* or *believe*, or descriptive adjectives. An opinion is called a **subjective** statement.

A. Read the advertisement again. List all the objective and subjective statements under the proper headings below.

Objective Statements

____

____

____

Subjective Statements

____

____

____

____

____

B. Change each objective statement below to a subjective statement. The first one has been done as an example.

1. Queen Elizabeth I of England never married.

   It was smart of Queen Elizabeth I of England never to marry.

2. The tax rate rose last year.

   ____

3. Vitamin C is found in citrus fruit.

   ____

4. Willie Mays was elected to the Hall of Fame in 1979.

   ____

5. The Beatles first toured the United States in 1964.

   ____

6. Dentists x-ray, repair, and clean teeth.

   ____

C. Change each subjective statement below to an objective statement. Remember to use only facts.

1. You shouldn't drink most cola drinks, since they contain caffeine.

____

2. Hawaii, our fiftieth state, is surely the most beautiful.

____

3. The Concorde may fly faster than the speed of sound, but it is too noisy.

____

4. I hate turnips even though they contain vitamins A, B complex, and C.

____

5. Of the twenty-six major league baseball teams, the Yankees have the best players.

____

We find much objective writing in newspapers and news magazines. **News stories** give facts that tell who, what, when, where, why, and how. News articles usually do not include opinions. Opinions can be found on the editorial pages and in reviews. Subjective writing is also found in **feature stories.** Features may be humorous or personal columns, or they may give background information about an event, including interviews.

D. Look at each headline or title below. Decide whether the article it describes is an objective, news-type article or a subjective article. Write *O* or *S* after each.

1. FIRE DESTROYS WAREHOUSE ______
2. WHY I'D LIKE TO VISIT THE MOON ______
3. SENATE VOTES TAX CUT ______
4. NEW ACTRESS EXCELLENT IN STARRING ROLE ______
5. BO GRANOWSKI—BEST CANDIDATE FOR MAYOR ______
6. NEW PLANET DISCOVERED ______

E. Write a news story for your school paper. Is there a special event you'd like to report on? If not, pretend that your lunchroom has just served its millionth meal. Write a short news article describing the location, the food, what time meals are served, and any other facts of interest to a reader. Remember to state only the facts.

____

____

____

F. Now write a subjective article about the event you described in part **E.** If you wrote about the lunchroom, you may wish to write an editorial about the food, the atmosphere, the prices, or anything else connected with the lunchroom.

Write On

Conduct a survey among several of your friends. Decide on one current-event topic to ask their opinions of. You may choose to ask about their favorite sports figure or TV show or their opinions on a local issue, such as pollution. Ask one or two questions, and take notes on the answers. Then write an feature article containing the results of your survey. You may wish to include your own thoughts about the survey in the article.

An objective article contains only facts. A subjective article expresses the writer's feelings and opinions.

lesson

2 Writing a research report

"Quick! Break a forked branch off that tree over there so I can catch this king snake. I need it for a demonstration at the Science Fair."

Ramón ran over to where Walt was pointing to a small snake with red, yellow, and black stripes running around its body. "That's not a king snake, you ninny!" he shouted. "It's a coral snake, and it's deadly poisonous!"

"Oh, come off it," sneered Walt. "Everybody knows that the coral snake has the bands of color separated by the black and the king snake is the other way around."

"I'm sure you're wrong," said Ramón. "Besides, the king snake is a big snake, and this one is little."

"Well, maybe it's a baby," said Walt.

While the boys were arguing, the king (or coral) snake, frightened by the shouting, slithered into the bushes and disappeared, leaving the boys time enough to look up the differences between king and coral snakes in the "Snakes" section of the encyclopedia.

An **encyclopedia** is a book or set of books containing factual articles on various topics. It is a reliable source of information and a good place to begin researching a topic. Several other reliable sources of information are listed below.

A **dictionary:** word meanings, spellings, pronunciations, origins
A **newspaper** or **news magazine:** current events
A **professional journal:** specific, up-to-date information in one field
A **textbook:** information on one subject
An **almanac** or **yearbook:** yearly events
A **who's who:** information about famous people
A **book of quotations:** famous quotations
A **biography:** facts about a specific person

A. Next to each question below, indicate the source you would use to locate the answer. You may list more than one source for each question.

1. What is tomorrow's weather forecast? ______________________

2. What country produces the most zinc? ______________________

3. What is the derivation of the word *automation*? ______________________

4. Who said "I only regret that I have but one life to lose for my country"?

____

5. In what year was Jimmy Carter born? ______________________

6. What events lead to the outbreak of World War I? ______________________

7. Which baseball team won the 1977 World Series? ______________________

8. Where were the major cities of ancient Egypt located? ______________________

9. What recent discoveries have been made in the field of cancer research?

____

10. When did Beverly Sills make her operatic debut? ______________________

Students are often asked to write research papers or reports. The word *report* means "carry back." When you write a report, you carry back information to your reader.

A good way to start researching a report is to select a manageable topic, one that can be fully covered in a limited amount of space.

B. Look at each pair of topics that follow. Which one is more narrow? Put a check mark next to the topic in each pair that can be covered in a short report.

1. ______ a. The U.S. Space Program

______ b. The First Astronauts on the Moon

2. _______ a. How Guide Dogs for the Blind Are Trained

_______ b. Animals That Help People

3. _______ a. American Artists

_______ b. The Art of Georgia O'Keeffe

4. _______ a. Underwater Life

_______ b. How to Scuba Dive

5. _______ a. The 1978 World Series

_______ b. The Game of Baseball

C. Now you try it. For each broad topic below, think of at least two more narrow topics. Write them on the lines provided.

1. Food

____

____

2. Criminals

____

____

3. Wild Animals

____

____

When you have a manageable topic, you have to decide what specific information on the topic you will need.

D. Choose one of the topics you wrote for part **C.** Think of at least three questions about the topic that you would like answers for. Then tell what sources you will use to find answers.

Topic: ______________________________

Questions: ______________________________

____

____

Sources for answers: ______________________________

____

When you have gathered the facts, arrange them in a logical order. An outline will help you. Begin your report with a clearly written introductory paragraph that states the questions you hope to answer in the report.

E. Use the lines below for your outline. You may fill in part of it now or wait until you have done some research on your topic. Turn back to Unit 1, Lesson 2, pages 6–9 if you need help outlining.

____

____

____

____

____

____

Write On

Research the topic you chose for part **D.** Write or complete your outline for part **E.** Then, on another sheet or two, write a short report on your topic. Don't forget the introductory paragraph.

A research report contains factual information on a topic. A good report follows a logical order and begins with an introductory paragraph.

Writing an ad

a.

b.

More and more people are switching to
LEAN LOOK.
Why? One look will tell you.

c.

You may not like to think so, but it's still true that "clothes make the man."
They may cost a little more, but they're worth it.
HENRI'S HABERDASHERY
Makers of fine men's clothing since 1898.

d.

Sale! Sale! Sale!
Loony Laurie's Lingerie
Laurie must be out of her mind—
Three pairs of stockings for the price of one!
Come get them while they last!

e.

Mrs. Marcia Steinway, a housewife in Bayonne, New Jersey, says,
"I never knew how clean floors could be until I used **Strip 'n' Shine**!"
Be good to yourself! Try some today!

f. More dentists use GLISTEN on their own teeth!
What better recommendation could there be?

g. Tired? Rundown? Depressed?
Why not get **Perk-Up?**
Puts a spring in your step
and a gleam in your eye!

h. Grandma never counted the apples she put in her pies.
And we don't either.
Buy farm-fresh, deep-dish **Gran's Apple Pies.**

What soap do you use? Where do you buy your clothes? Do you take pills when you get a cold?

Smart consumers look for the facts. Smart ad writers may use facts as part of their ads, but they often try to get you to buy something by using techniques which appeal more to your emotions than to your mind.

A. Which ads on these pages use the techniques described below? Write the letter of the ad in front of the description of each technique.

______ 1. **Loaded Words.** Plus-loaded words like *stylish, slender,* and *beautiful* are often used to describe the product or how you will feel or look using the product. Minus-loaded words like *embarrassed, unattractive,* and *worried* are often used to describe how you must look or feel without the product. Loaded words appeal to your hopes and fears.

______ 2. **Down Home.** Some people feel that things were better in the good old days down home on the farm. Words like *natural, fresh, home-baked,* and *healthful* are often used to describe products with such names as "Aunt Hattie's Cookie Jar Natural Oatmeal Cookies."

______ 3. **Bandwagon Method.** These ads try to make you feel that everyone is jumping on the "bandwagon" to do something (and that you'll be missing something terrific if you don't go along). Such ads say things like "Four out of five mothers choose Silky Dry disposable diapers" and "Sixteen million people in California loved it."

______ 4. **Snob Appeal.** These ads appeal to people's desires to feel special, important, or "high class." They use such phrases as "for men who care about their looks" and "It costs more, but it's worth it."

______ 5. **Just Plain Folks.** These ads show ordinary people doing ordinary things. Manufacturers hope we will identify with these "just plain folks" and trust their recommendations.

______ 6. **Celebrities.** When famous people recommend products, some of their glamor is supposed to rub off on the products and make us want them more.

______ 7. **Experts.** These ads use actors dressed as doctors, auto mechanics, and other experts whose word we would be likely to trust.

______ 8. **Bargains.** If a price tag says "Value: $10.00; Sale Price: $6.50," people will be more likely to buy the product than if it said simply "$6.50." Everyone loves a bargain.

Did you notice that most of the ads on page 74 include a catchy name and slogan? A **slogan** is a phrase or sentence used repeatedly, such as "the little car that's big on value."

B. New products are invented every day. The marketing of a product is often just as important to its success as the product itself. What names and slogans can you think of for these new products?

1. A computer that lets you select your groceries at home

Name: ______________________________

Slogan: ______________________________

2. A new kind of clay (Think of something special about it.)

Name: ______________________________

Slogan: ______________________________

3. A wireless portable telephone

Name: ______________________________

Slogan: ______________________________

4. A magazine for bowling enthusiasts

Name: ______________________________

Slogan: ______________________________

5. A book for junior high students with tips on how to get along in school

Name: ______________________________

Slogan: ______________________________

6. An educational toy (What does it teach?)

Name: ______________________________

Slogan: ______________________________

7. A mouthwash

Name: ______________________________

Slogan: ______________________________

C. Now pick one of the products above and write an ad for it. Use the product name, a slogan, and one or more of the techniques described in part **A.** How the ad looks is just as important as what it says. Make a sketch for the ad or describe how you would like to have it illustrated.

____

Think of a product that needs inventing. On another sheet of paper, design an ad campaign to sell your product. Invent a name and a slogan. Describe the kind of ad you will use to sell your product on TV. Also write and illustrate a magazine ad for your product.

The purpose of ads is to try to influence consumers to buy products. Ads often appeal to our emotions. They may use the testimony of celebrities, experts, or just plain folks. They also may use loaded words, the bandwagon method, snob appeal, or the down home appeal, or they may appeal to our love of bargains.

Revising

Using specific nouns and verbs

A good writer reports the facts clearly and accurately. One way to say exactly what you mean is to use specific nouns and verbs in your writing. Compare the sentences below.

The woman tried to get elected.
Angela J. Thomasini campaigned for senator.

A. Next to each general noun below, write three specific nouns.

1. animal ______ ______ ______
2. food ______ ______ ______
3. vehicle ______ ______ ______
4. person ______ ______ ______
5. building ______ ______ ______

B. Each sentence below can be made more specific. On the line after each sentence, write a specific noun to replace each underlined vague word.

1. The children's <u>things</u> were scattered across the lawn. ______
2. A movie doesn't seem complete without <u>food</u>. ______
3. The flood waters damaged many <u>buildings</u>. ______
4. Certainly <u>they</u> will volunteer to work at the hospital. ______
5. The <u>animal</u> stalked its prey. ______

Choosing specific verbs can also help your writing. One specific verb can often do the job of a vague verb and adverb. Compare these sentences.

Vague: Vincent went quickly.
Better: Vincent ran (or raced).

C. Next to each general verb that follows, write three specific verbs.

1. say ______ ______ ______
2. see ______ ______ ______
3. work ______ ______ ______

D. Revise each sentence below by replacing the underlined word or words with a more specific verb.

1. The puppy cried in pain. ______________________________

2. The snow fell slowly to the earth. ______________________________

3. We ate our lunch hurriedly. ______________________________

4. The thief looked at the police officer with anger. ______________________________

E. The sentence below is vague.

The person liked the thing.

Revise the sentence to make it clearer and more accurate. Then use it as the topic sentence of a paragraph. Add several sentences of your own. Remember to use specific nouns and verbs.

____

____

____

____

____

____

____

Write On

Look at the "Write On" papers you have completed for this unit. Choose one to revise. Make it more accurate and clear by using specific nouns and verbs.

Use specific nouns and verbs to make your sentences clear and accurate.

Post-Test

1. Next to each statement below, write S if you think it should appear in a subjective article and O if you think it should appear in an objective article.

_____ a. "That's My Family" is the best new show on TV this fall.

_____ b. On January 1st, the Central Railroad will raise fares by 30%.

_____ c. Summer passes in a flash, but winter seems to last forever.

_____ d. Sweden has not been at war for more than 160 years.

_____ e. During the Middle Ages, no two knights could have the same coat of arms.

2. Which of the topics below would be most suitable for a two-page research report? State your reasons on the lines.

a. The American West b. My Favorite TV Westerns c. The Santa Fe Trail

____

____

3. Match each ad phrase with the technique it illustrates.

_____ Mrs. Bird's Puddings have that country kitchen taste.	a. loaded words
_____ For those who value excellence.	b. bargain pitch
_____ Our low, low prices have been slashed in half!	c. snob appeal
_____ In times of uncertainty, you need a bank you can trust.	d. down home

4. Next to each general word write three specific words.

a. machine _____________ _____________ _____________

b. toy _____________ _____________ _____________

c. walk _____________ _____________ _____________

d. laugh _____________ _____________ _____________

5. Write two paragraphs about one of the topics below. In the first paragraph, include only objective statements. In the second paragraph, include only subjective statements.

My Home Town My Favorite Book A Job for the Future

unit 6

Making Your Point in Writing

Things to Remember About Making Your Point in Writing

The **purpose** of a piece of writing may be to inform, to entertain, to express feelings or opinions, or to persuade.

Writing

- Use formal diction, informal diction, or slang to fit the purpose of your writing.
- Write better persuasive articles by basing your opinions on facts, presenting your viewpoint clearly, and telling why you disagree with opposing viewpoints. Prepare the article by listing the facts and arguments both for and against the issue.
- Write a letter of complaint as a business letter with two parts. Make one part explain the problem and the second part suggest a solution.

Revising

- Give your paragraphs better rhythm by combining sentences, removing repetitious words, and varying your sentence structure.

lesson

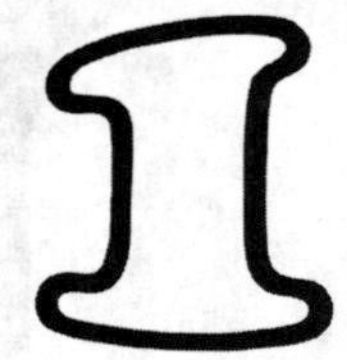

Using formal and informal diction

Mr. and Mrs. J. Worthmore Doe
request the honor of your presence
at the marriage of their daughter

Lotta

to

Mr. I. Ned Cash

on Saturday, the first of January

at twelve o'clock noon.

Reception following the ceremony
at the King Midas Country Club.

R.S.V.P.

January 1st

SATURDAY NITE BASH
Dogs! Burgers! Pop!

Disco Dancing!

Bring a friend!

Bring a record!

Bring a buck!

Bennie's pad – 7 till ???

As you can see from the invitations above, two very different parties are taking place on January 1. Each invitation uses **diction,** or word choice, appropriate to the occasion.

Look at the two sentences below. The first sentence uses **formal diction.** The second sentence uses **informal diction.** Notice the difference in the choice of words.

Would you care to accompany me to the motion pictures this evening?
Let's go to the movies tonight.

A. Find samples of formal and informal diction in the invitations at the top of the page. List the words you find in the proper columns below. The first examples have been done for you.

Formal Diction	Informal Diction
request	nite

Your choice of diction depends on what you are writing and whom it is for. In a letter to a close friend, your writing can be as informal as you wish. In a letter to someone you don't know well, you would express yourself more formally. In a letter to a close friend or relative, the greeting and closing, as well as the body, will often be quite informal. Compare the diction of these greetings and closings.

Formal	**Informal**
Dear Mrs. Wentworth,	Howdy, Soupy!
Sincerely yours,	See ya!

B. Choose one of the occasions below or think of a real occasion. Write an informal letter on the lines below. (Page 124 in the Handbook shows the form for a friendly letter.)

1. Write to a real or imaginary friend inviting him or her to a Halloween party that has something special about it. Be sure to mention the time and place.
2. You borrowed your cousin's original collection of Superman comics and your dog chewed them up. Write a letter to your cousin explaining what happened and thinking of some way you can make it up to her or him.

____________________ Heading

____

____

Greeting ____________________

Body ____

____________________ Closing

____________________ Signature

C. Your little sister took all the cards off your birthday presents, and you don't know who sent which gift. Your wealthy great-aunt, whom you have never met, expects a thank-you note. Write her a letter using more formal diction than your letter in part **B.**

We usually use informal diction in conversations. If you are writing dialogue for a story, try to make it sound natural.

D. Read this rather stilted conversation. On the lines below, rewrite it using more informal diction.

James: I am planning to dine at Ye Olde Tea Shoppe today at noon. May I have the pleasure of your company?

William: I will be delighted to join you for the midday repast, and I thank you kindly for the invitation. Perhaps we can stroll downtown afterward. I have an important engagement at two.

James: Certainly. I shall be happy to accompany you.

Informal diction and **slang,** which includes colorful words and invented expressions, can make language lively. Read this passage.

> I got so bushed mowing the lawn, I didn't see that pop bottle that totaled the power mower. Then my old man knocked five bucks off my allowance for the damages, and when I gave him a little static, he not only grounded me—he said I couldn't borrow his heap for Bennie's brawl. I said, "Dad, what kind of jazz is that? You know I can't make the scene without wheels."
>
> "Tell it to the Marines," he said. "Bennie's pad is only four blocks away. You can hoof it."

E. If you had some friends who were just learning English, how would you "translate" the passage above for them? Rewrite the passage on the lines below. Avoid slang and use slightly more formal diction.

Write On You would like to find a summer job. Write an informal letter to your uncle asking for work in his store. Write a second, more formal, letter to the Personnel Manager of Hill's Department Store. (Page 123 in the Handbook shows the form for a business letter.)

Use formal diction, informal diction, or slang to fit the purpose of your writing.

lesson

2 Writing a persuasive article

A. In the picture above, people are considering the **pros** and **cons** of doing various things. *Pro* is a Latin word meaning "for." *Con* (short for *contra*) means "against." What decisions do the people in the picture need to make?

____

____

____

B. Just for fun, write a short argument in favor of each of the items below.

1. Castor oil: ______________________________

____

2. Measles shots: ______________________________

____

3. Making your bed: ______________________________

____

4. Flies: ______________________________

____

5. Banana skins: ______________________________

____

C. Now, give one argument against each of these.

1. Mouthwash: ______________________________

____

2. TV: ______________________________

____

3. Cupcakes: ______________________________

____

4. Disco dancing: ______________________________

____

5. Sunshine: ______________________________

____

Arguments for or against issues are often given in longer kinds of persuasive writing, such as essays and editorials. A persuasive article will be more convincing if it is based on facts.

One good way to prepare a persuasive article on an issue is to list the facts and arguments both for and against the issue.

D. List all the pros and cons you can for each of the following topics.

1. Everyone should be required to remain in school for twelve years.

Pro	Con
______________________	______________________
______________________	______________________
______________________	______________________
______________________	______________________
______________________	______________________
______________________	______________________

2. I would join a club which would not admit a good friend.

Pro	Con
______________________	______________________
______________________	______________________
______________________	______________________
______________________	______________________
______________________	______________________
______________________	______________________

3. If I won $50,000 in a lottery, I would put it all in a bank.

Pro	Con
______________________	______________________
______________________	______________________
______________________	______________________
______________________	______________________
______________________	______________________
______________________	______________________

Recognizing both the pros and cons of an issue can help you write a better persuasive article. Not only will you present your own viewpoint more clearly, but you will be in a better position to defend yourself against the opposition's arguments.

E. Select one of the topics from part **D.** Decide which viewpoint you will present in a persuasive article. You can organize the article in one of two ways. The first way is to present all the "pros" in the first paragraph, to defend yourself against opposing viewpoints in the second paragraph, and to sum up your arguments in a final sentence or paragraph. The second way is to alternate specific pros and cons as you go along, showing the strength of each "pro" and the weakness of each "con." Here again, it's a good idea to restate your point of view at the end.

____

____

____

____

____

____

____

____

____

____

____

____

____

____

____

Write On

Should there be capital punishment? The issue of whether or not the state should execute people for their crimes has been the focus of many debates. You may wish to research the existing arguments and decide which viewpoint you support. Then write a persuasive article on capital punishment, either pro or con. Remember to state your arguments clearly and to tell why you disagree with the opposing viewpoints.

A good persuasive article is based on facts, presents the writer's viewpoint clearly, and tells why the writer disagrees with opposing viewpoints.

lesson 3

Writing a letter of complaint

A. Has this ever happened to you? Tell about an experience you or a friend had when you returned something to a store.

____

____

____

____

If you have a complaint about something you've bought, you can usually return it to the store where you purchased it. However, if the store will not take the item back, or if you have ordered something by mail, the best way to protest is to write a **letter of complaint** to the manufacturer.

Look at the following letters of complaint.

2 Windy Heights
Cold Corner, Vermont
August 29, 19—

President
Bushy Top Hair Restorer, Inc.
100 Smooth Pate Road
Bald Eagle, Utah

Dear President:

I have been using your hair restorer for three weeks, and I'm balder than ever. Then I reread your ad: "Guaranteed to make hair grow on a billiard ball." So I tried it on a billiard ball. My billiard ball now has hair, but I don't. What do you expect me to do? My head is cold without hair, and it's hard to play billiards when the ball doesn't roll properly.

Sincerely yours,
Laun Maurer
Laun Maurer

3 Cowlick Road
Hartoff, Texas
August 29, 19—

President
Bushy Top Hair Restorer, Inc.
100 Smooth Pate Road
Bald Eagle, Utah

Dear President:

On August 2 I sent you a check for $12.95 for three bottles of Bushy Top Hair Restorer, guaranteed, your ad said, to restore hair in three weeks. In the last three weeks I have used all three bottles, but I still have no hair.

I would like a full refund on my purchase. Thank you.

Sincerely yours,
Curly Wunss
Curly Wunss

B. Compare the two letters of complaint. Which one do you think is more effective, and why?

___

___

___

An effective letter of complaint has two parts. The first part gives the facts about what was bought and what was wrong with it. The second part tells how you would like to have the problem resolved.

C. You have just bought a new three-speed chopper, but it doesn't work properly. Write a letter to the president of the General Specific Corporation, 104 Over View, Fax, Kansas, to complain about your new chopper. First, state what the chopper is supposed to do and what is wrong with it. Then tell the president what you want the company to do about it. This is a business letter, so remember to use an inside address and a colon after the greeting. Print your letter clearly.

D. Have you or has anyone you know ever bought something defective? Make a list of the unsatisfactory products here.

____

____

____

____

Defective products are not the only reason to write a letter of complaint. Think about problems that cause inconvenience or hardship to people in your school or community, such as pollution, parking, traffic. A letter of complaint sent to an editor of a local newspaper, your mayor, or a local representative can bring these problems to the attention of people who are in a position to change things.

E. Have you noticed any problems in your community or school? Make a list of the problems here.

____

____

____

____

Choose one of the problems you listed in part **D** or part **E.** On another sheet of paper, write a letter of complaint to the proper person. Explain the problem and suggest a solution. Remember to use correct business letter form.

A letter of complaint is a business letter with two parts. One part explains the problem. The second part suggests a solution.

lesson 4

Revising

Sentence and paragraph rhythm

Both groups below begin a Mayan story about creation.

God wanted to make a man. The man would be the first man. God made the man out of mud.

When God wanted to make the first man, He made him out of mud.

Notice how the three short sentences have been combined into one longer, smoother sentence. In the longer sentence, some of the repeated words were eliminated, and the connection between the sentences was made clearer by addition of the word *when*.

A. The following sentences continue the Mayan story. Combine each group in a way that seems both smoother and clearer.

1. The mud was too soft. The man kept falling down. The man kept dissolving into the earth.

   ____

   ____

2. Then God made another man. He made the man out of wood. This man did not fall down. This man did not dissolve.

   ____

   ____

3. This man was stiff. This man was inflexible. This man stood there. This man looked stupid.

   ____

   ____

4. Then God took cornmeal dough. God shaped a man. God baked the man firm in the sun.

   ____

   ____

5. The man was pliant. The man was golden brown. That was the shape that all men took forever after.

Generally, a paragraph reads well if the sentences don't all begin the same way and if their lengths vary. Too many short, choppy sentences spoil a paragraph's rhythm.

B. Here is an adaptation of a fable by Aesop, called "The Dog in the Manger." Rewrite it on the lines below. Combine sentences to make the story read more smoothly.

A dog was looking for a place. The place was for an afternoon nap. The dog jumped into a manger. The manger belonged to an ox. The dog lay there. The dog lay upon the straw. It was cozy. Soon the ox returned from its work. The ox came up to the manger. The ox wanted to eat some straw. The dog was awakened from its slumber. The dog was in a rage. The dog stood up. The dog barked at the ox. The ox came near. The dog tried to bite it. The ox gave up hope. Its hope was to get at the straw. The ox went away. The ox muttered, "People often will not let others enjoy things. They cannot enjoy those things themselves."

Write On

Look over your papers for this unit and see which ones have paragraphs with a choppy rhythm. Select one and revise the paragraph on a separate piece of paper. Remember to change or omit repetitious words and to combine sentences.

Your paragraphs will have better rhythm if you combine sentences, avoid repetitious words, and vary sentence structure.

Post-Test

1. Rewrite the passage below. Avoid slang and use more formal diction.

Dan and I bugged Mom to spring for the bucks for the movies, but she wouldn't come across with the dough unless we whipped our bedroom into shape. The room was a horror show and was really freaking her out. We busted our backs but finished the job.

____

____

____

____

2. Write one argument for and one argument against this statement: Every student should be required to join one sports team.

Pro: ____________________________________

Con: ____________________________________

3. Combine these short choppy sentences to make them read more smoothly.

The fox was hungry. The fox wanted some grapes. The grapes were on a high vine. The fox jumped for the grapes. He jumped again. He jumped again. The fox couldn't reach the grapes. He gave up. "Those grapes are sour. They are bitter," he said.

____

____

____

4. Write two persuasive paragraphs on one of the topics below. Or, you can choose your own topic. In the first paragraph, give arguments for the statement. In the second paragraph, give arguments against the statement.

Cigarette and cigar smoking should be banned.

Gym classes should not be required in school.

A student should be allowed to sit in any seat in a classroom.

unit 7
Point of View in Writing

Things to Remember About Point of View in Your Writing

A **point of view** is the way someone sees, thinks, or feels about something.

Writing Tips

- Imagine how things seem from one or more characters' points of view. Then decide on the point of view you will use in a story.
- Use a first-person narrator when you want to have everything in the story experienced from the narrator's point of view. Use *I, me,* and *my.*
- Use the third-person subjective point of view when you want to report the action mainly from one person's point of view without having that person narrate the story.
- Use the third-person omniscient point of view when you want to explain more than one person's thoughts, feelings, and motives.
- Choose the genre that best expresses the point of view you want to use: play, poem, short story, essay, or news article.

Revising

Revise your writing by

- adding adverbs
- combining sentences
- cutting out repetitious, misplaced, or dangling modifiers
- using specific adjectives, verbs, and nouns
- varying sentence structure

lesson

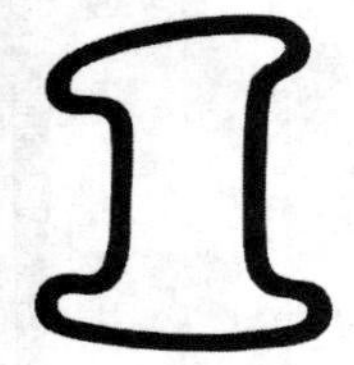

Writing about an event from different views

The Queen of Hearts,
She made some tarts,
All on a summer's day.

The Knave of Hearts,
He stole those tarts
And took them clean away

The King of Hearts
Called for the tarts
And beat the knave full sore.

The Knave of Hearts
Brought back the tarts
And vowed he'd steal no more.

These few lines from a famous Mother Goose rhyme tell a whole story. You can use your imagination to fill in the details, such as:

1. What kind of tarts were they?
2. Why did the knave steal them?
3. How did he do it?
4. How did the queen feel about the theft?
5. How did the king find out who did it?
6. How did the characters feel about the knave's punishment?

One of the most important skills a writer needs to develop is the ability to get into the mind of each character and to imagine how things seem from his or her **point of view.**

People sometimes record their thoughts and feelings in a **diary.** A person's diary gives a brief daily account of things that have happened that the person wants to remember.

A. Imagine you are one of the characters in the nursery rhyme on page 98. On the lines below, write what you might have written in your diary on the day the tarts were stolen.

Diary of ______________________________ (character)

B. Now tell the story from the point of view of a different character. What would that person's diary say?

Diary of ______________________________ (character)

FIERY COMET STILL APPROACHING

Washington, D.C., December 20. Concerned citizens today began organizing a total evacuation campaign as the unidentified comet that has threatened the earth for five days moved closer at a steady rate. Scientists and technicians from every field are being questioned about any possibility, however remote, that the population of this planet will be able to escape or survive the unimaginable shock that would accompany a collision.

C. Suppose you read the story above in your morning newspaper. What would you write in your diary? On the lines below, write about your thoughts and fears, your hopes for survival, and any ideas you have about how to save yourself and your family.

Everyone has fears, doubts, hopes, wishes, and thoughts, but each of us experiences them in her or his own personal way. Fiction writers use differences in the way a person reacts to an experience to bring their characters to life.

D. Choose one of the following characters to bring to life. Decide what thoughts and fears about the threatening comet would be uppermost in that person's mind. On the lines below, write his or her diary entry about the comet.

the parent of six youngsters	a religious leader
a police officer	a doctor
the President of the United States	a person in a wheelchair
Superman or Wonder Woman	a scientist

Write On

Choose another of the characters listed in part **D.** On one or two separate sheets of paper, write that person's diary entry about the comet.

An important writing skill is the ability to imagine how things seem from one or more characters' points of view.

lesson

2 Writing first-person and third-person narratives

When a writer tells a story, that story is called a **narrative.** In a **first-person narrative,** the narrator is (or pretends to be) the subject of the story and uses the words *I, me, my,* and *mine.* Everything that happens in the story is experienced from the narrator's point of view.

In a **third-person narrative,** each character is referred to as *she* or *he* or by name. There is no *I, me, my,* or *mine,* except in quotations. The writer may or may not tell the story from one character's point of view.

Look at the difference below.

Third Person: The Queen of Hearts made some tarts.
First Person: I made some tarts.

A. Read each story beginning below. On the blank line in front of each, write *FP* if it is a first-person narrative or *TP* if it is a third-person narrative.

______ 1. No one who had ever seen Catherine Morland in her infancy would have supposed her born to be a heroine. (Jane Austen, *Northanger Abbey*)

______ 2. The thousand injuries of Fortunato I had borne as best as I could; but when he ventured upon insult, I vowed revenge. (Edgar Allan Poe, "The Cask of Amontillado")

______ 3. You don't know about me without you have read a book by the name of *The Adventures of Tom Sawyer,* but that ain't no matter. (Mark Twain, *The Adventures of Huckleberry Finn*)

______ 4. As Mr. John Oakhurst, gambler, stepped into the main street of Poker Flat on the morning of the 23rd of November, 1850, he was conscious of a change in its moral atmosphere since the preceding night. (Bret Harte, "The Outcasts of Poker Flat")

______ 5. Whether I shall turn out to be the hero of my own life or whether that station will be held by anybody else, these pages must show. (Charles Dickens, *David Copperfield*)

Read this first-person narrative.

"Last one in's a rotten egg," I shouted as we ran to the edge of the quarry lake. I hesitated just for a second and then plunged in.

The cold water shocked me wide awake as it closed over my head. As I waited for my body to stop going down and start coming up, I remembered that we'd come because Toni dared me to race her out to the rock. I got to the surface just as she dived off the bank. She hit the water and went down. I must have counted a hundred bubbles before her head finally bobbed to the surface. Then I saw her face. She was grinning and pointing at the huge granite rock sticking up in the middle of the lake.

I swam toward the rock until my arms ached, gulping down stinging mouthfuls of quarry water, half of it through my nose. Would I make it through the blasthole? It was six feet under the surface of the lake. No one had ever swum through it before. Then I realized that in that moment before Toni came up, I almost wished that something awful had happened to her. Why had I taken her dare? Why did she make me feel this way?

B. Rewrite the passage above as a third-person narrative. Give the narrator a name and describe what happened without using *I*, *me*, or *my*.

____

____

____

____

____

____

____

____

____

____

____

____

Two kinds of third person narratives are **subjective** and **omniscient.** In a subjective third-person narrative, the action is reported mainly from the point of view of just one person in the story. In an omniscient (all-knowing) third-person narrative, the narrator takes no part in the story, but seems to know how all the characters act, think, and feel.

Read this news article.

FREMONT, February 27—Among the four men apprehended in yesterday's attempted hold-up of the Freemont National Bank was Toby ("Turtle") Tarragon, the reputed leader of a criminal ring that has been successfully robbing many banks in the area.

Mark Spillman, head of the Criminal Investigation Unit that arrested the hold-up men, said, "We haven't made such an important catch in years. We are proud of our force."

C. Use the information in the news article above as the basis for a paragraph of a cops-and-robbers story in the subjective third person. Tell it from the point of view of the police officer, Mark Spillman. Keep the reader in the same suspenseful state as Spillman so that your reader, like Spillman, never knows exactly what the robbers are planning to do next. Continue the paragraph started below.

Mark Spillman spoke into his walkie-talkie. "It was the Turtle, Chief," ______

______

______

______

D. Now use the same characters and situation to write two paragraphs for another story in the omniscient third person. In the first paragraph, use the third person to tell where Toby Tarragon is and what his thoughts, feelings, and motives are the morning before the robbery. In the second paragraph, continue the third-person narrative, but change locations and tell about Mark Spillman's thoughts and feelings as he gets ready for another day.

Paragraph 1: ______

Paragraph 2: ______

Write On

Choose one of the characters in this lesson—one of the swimmers on page 103, Mark Spillman, or Toby ("Turtle") Tarragon. Write a short story about this character, using the events described in this lesson or a completely different event. Decide whether your story will be a first-person, third-person subjective, or third-person omniscient narrative. Once you have chosen the point of view, be consistent.

A narrative may be written from the first person, third-person subjective, or third-person omniscient point of view, depending on the writer's goals.

lesson

3 Writing in different forms

Sometimes, when an emergency strikes, people rise to the occasion. These commuters, stranded in a subway tunnel for over two hours, managed to keep each other's spirits up, as you can see from the picture.

This event, or a similar one, might inspire several writers. Each writer might choose a different **genre,** or form of writing, to express her or his thoughts.

A. Write about the stalled train. Choose one of the following genres. Use the lines below.

1. An editorial for the local paper condemning the poor subway conditions that caused the train to stall (Recommend action that needs to be taken.)
2. A feature article for the newspaper telling how the passengers spent their time (Include statements by two or three passengers.)
3. A song about the incident (Think of lines for the refrain or chorus that give the idea of the song. It could be a love song, a song about the people on the train, a song about the hardships of city living, or something else.)
4. Notes for a story—a mystery,a love story, a story of foiled plans,or something else (Include the conflict and resolution.)
5. A letter from someone who was on the train to a friend who wasn't, describing the experience with enthusiasm or disgust
6. A poem based on the incident (Perhaps each line might tell what each passenger was thinking about when the train stalled.)

One incident can inspire reactions in several different genres, depending on the goals of the writer. Often something written in one genre will inspire a writer to adapt it to another genre. Shakespeare got the ideas for his plays from tales and histories that were popular at the time. And many movies are based on stories or novels.

Stories may be told from one character's point of view, giving the thoughts and feelings of that character. They often include descriptive passages. A playwright, on the other hand, uses only dialogue and stage directions to make the plot of a story clear. Look at these examples from *Through the Looking-Glass.*

Story Form

"Where do you come from?" said the Red Queen. "And where are you going? Look up; speak nicely, and don't twiddle your fingers all the time."

Alice attended to all these directions, and explained, as well as she could, that she had lost her way.

Play Form

RED QUEEN: Where do you come from? And where are you going? Look up, speak nicely, and don't twiddle your fingers all the time.

ALICE *(looking up and keeping her fingers still):* I'm afraid I have lost my way.

B. Try your hand at adapting the following scene from *Alice's Adventures in Wonderland* for a musical. Copy or adapt (change slightly) the words Alice and the Cheshire Cat say. Then, at some point, have Alice or the cat or both break into song. If you have trouble thinking of lyrics for a song, write down an idea for what the song could be about. The passage that follows begins when Alice asks a question of the Cheshire Cat, who is sitting in a tree near her.

"What sort of people live about here?"

"In that direction," the Cat said, waving its right paw around, "lives a Hatter; and in that direction," waving the other paw, "lives a March Hare. Visit either you like: they're both mad."

"But I don't want to go among mad people," Alice remarked.

Oh, you can't help that," said the Cat; "we're all mad here. I'm mad. You're mad."

"How do you know I'm mad?" said Alice.

"You must be," said the Cat, "or you wouldn't have come here."

Alice didn't think that proved it at all; however, she went on. "And how do you know that you're mad?"

"To begin with," said the Cat, "a dog's not mad. You grant that?"

"I suppose so," said Alice.

"Well, then," the Cat went on, "you see a dog growls when it's angry, and wags its tail when it's pleased. Now I growl when I'm pleased, and wag my tail when I'm angry. Therefore I'm mad."

Dialogue: ____

____

____

____

____

____

____

____

____

____

____

____

____

____

Song: ____

____

____

____

Write On

Do one of the following:

1. Choose another genre from part **A** and write about the stalled train.
2. Choose a scene from a story you like and adapt it for a play or musical.

Writers can express their ideas and feelings in different forms, or genres.

Revising

lesson

Polishing your writing

Chances are that any piece of writing in any book you have read is the product of one or more revisions. Most writers write, read, cross out, rewrite, type, reread, and revise their work until it says what they want it to say. For some people this is a quick process, for others a long one.

A. The rules below review some of the guidelines for revising what you have studied in this book. Use them to help you revise the sentences beneath each rule.

1. Add adverbs to sentences to give specific information about how, when, and where.

   The couple danced.

   ____

   ____

2. Use coordinate and subordinate conjunctions and conjunctive adverbs to combine short, choppy sentences and to show relationships of events.

   The spaceship went off without her. The astronaut had to make her home on the strange planet. She remembered she had some seed packets in her back pocket. She decided to plant the seeds.

   ____

   ____

   ____

3. Don't overload your sentences with too many repetitious modifiers.

   The restless, squirming, bored audience squirmed and fidgeted through the dull, boring, uninteresting speech.

   ____

4. Rewrite sentences to correct misplaced or dangling modifiers.

   Shattered into a thousand pieces, Ludwig swept up the broken vase.

   ____

   Aunt Matilda bought a new vase, smiling broadly.

   ____

5. Use specific adjectives and details to make your sentences interesting and clear.

    The room looked strange. Paco felt funny.

____

____

6. Use specific nouns and verbs to make your sentences clear and accurate.

    They saw a lot of things down there.

____

____

7. Omit repeated words and vary sentence structure to improve paragraph rhythm.

    My little brother made breakfast. He made pancakes. The pancakes didn't taste very good. The pancakes were burned on one side. The pancakes were not cooked enough on the other side.

____

____

____

B. Revise the paragraph below, combining sentences and changing words until it sounds good to you.

The plane was going well. Suddenly, the pilot slumped over. The plane lurched. Spinning wildly, someone took the controls. The wild spinning stopped. It went straight again. It was smooth.

____

____

____

____

____

Write On

Go over all the papers you wrote this year and pick one that you think you could improve. Work on a revision, keeping in mind the guidelines you have studied in this book. Revise your paper until you feel satisfied that it sounds right and says what you want it to say. Then make a neat copy.

Revise your writing until it says exactly what you want it to say.

Post-Test

1. Read the rhyme. Then write a diary entry from the point of view of one character.

Jack and Jill went up the hill
To fetch a pail of water.
Jack fell down and broke his crown
And Jill came tumbling after.

Up Jack got and off did trot
As fast as he could caper
To old Dame Dobb who patched his knob
With vinegar and brown paper.

Diary of ______________________ : ______________________

____

____

2. Rewrite this passage from *David Copperfield* in third person.

"You aren't cross, I suppose, Peggotty, are you?" said I, after a minute.

I really thought she was, she had been so short with me; but I was quite mistaken: for she laid aside her work, and opening her arms wide, took my curly head within them, and gave it a good squeeze.

____

____

____

3. Adapt this passage from *Alice in Wonderland* as a play.

"Take some more tea," the March Hare said to Alice very earnestly.

"I've had nothing yet," Alice replied, offended, "so I can't take more."

"You mean you can't take less," said the Hatter. "It's very easy to take more than nothing."

____

____

____

4. Revise the paragraph to make it clearer and smoother.

The spaceship was huge. It was cigar-shaped. It landed. Creatures rushed out. With strangely glowing skulls, two teenagers watched them from a house.

____

____

5. In a diary entry, newspaper story, or play tell what the teenagers did after spotting the spaceship and creatures.

Writing Handbook

When your writing says exactly what you want it to say, it is a good idea to proofread to look for errors you might have made in capitalization, punctuation, or word usage. The following pages include rules for using capital letters, punctuation marks, and word forms correctly. Use this handbook as a reference whenever you have any questions. When you feel you know the rules, turn to page 124 and take the proofreading test there.

PART 1 **CAPITALIZATION**

1. The first word of every sentence begins with a capital letter.

   Who ate the pie? Find the pie!

   The first word of a direct quotation begins with a capital letter.

   I asked the class, "Who ate the pie?"
   They all replied, "No one."

2. In the titles or subtitles of works, the first, the last, and any important words begin with capital letters. "Important words" means all words except *a, an, the;* coordinate conjunctions; prepositions of four letters or under; and *to* in an infinitive.

   The Day of the Locust (book)
   A Night to Remember (film)
   The Last Supper (painting)
   the *Evening Gazette* (newspaper; *the* not part of title)

3. Every word or abbreviation in a proper noun begins with a capital letter (except *of, the, and*). A proper noun names a particular person, animal, place, or thing.

   Susan B. Anthony
   Paris, France (city/country)
   Lake George (body of water)
   Route 66 (road)
   the *Titanic* (boat)
   the Treaty of Ghent (document)
   Ajax cleanser (brand name)
   Tuesday, August 3 (day/month)
   Christmas (holiday)
   the First World War (historic event)
   Buddhism (religion)
   the FBI (organization)
   Winthrop High School (institution)
   the Republican Party (political party)
   the Debating Club (club)
   General Motors (company)

   Do not begin a common noun with a capital letter, even when it refers to a proper noun just mentioned. A common noun is a general noun (see page 120).

   We attend the university. I live in the state of Utah.
   We went to the Museum of Modern Art. The museum was closed.

4. Titles and ranks (and their abbreviations) begin with capital letters when they occur with names.

   Doctor K. Trombone　　Mr. George Fukuda, Jr.
   Aunt Anita　　Evelyn Frank, Ph.D.

   Ranks or titles that appear alone do not begin with capital letters.

   One of the generals came in.　　Where's my aunt?

   You may capitalize family relationship words that appear alone if they are used as names.

   Where is Auntie?　　She's with Mom.

5. Do not capitalize the words for directions unless they are being used as parts of names or to name specific geographic places.

   She went south.　　She lives on South Street.　　She visited the South.

PART 2 PUNCTUATION

Apostrophes (')

1. An apostrophe is used to show the possessive form of a noun.

   Joe's bike　　the girls' wagons　　the children's room

2. An apostrophe is used in a contraction to show that a letter or letters have been left out.

   won't (will not)　　can't (can not)　　it's (it is or it has)

Colons (:)

1. A colon is used to introduce a list.

   Please send the following items:

   one shirt　　two pairs sneakers　　one baseball bat

2. A colon is sometimes used to introduce a direct quotation (A comma would also be correct; a colon simply makes a stronger pause.)

   Alexander Pope said: "Whatever is, is right."

Commas (,)

1. A comma is used to separate two independent clauses linked by a coordinate conjunction.

   Leopold bought the tickets, and Marisa rented the car.

2. Commas are used to separate items in a series.

   He wore a coat, a sweater, three shirts, and a hat.

   It is not necessary to use commas in a series if coordinate conjunctions are used between all items.

   Wear a coat or a sweater or a jacket.

3. A comma is used to separate coordinate adjectives (adjectives of equal force that separately modify the same noun).

   Silvia is a tall, handsome woman.

   Do not use a comma to separate adjectives that are not coordinate.

   Ashley served the meal with typical Southern hospitality.

4. Commas are used to set off modifying phrases and clauses when they come before the main clause.

   To win, she worked hard.
   Falling down the steps, he dropped his books.
   Under a tree by the side of the river, the child slept.
   When I returned, home was no longer the same.

   A comma is not required after a short introductory adverbial phrase.

   Under a tree the child slept.

5. Commas are used to set off nonrestrictive modifying phrases and clauses. A nonrestrictive element is one that merely adds information to the word it follows.

   The defendant, fidgeting in the witness box, spoke.
   The snow, which was falling heavily, slowed our journey.
   We saw a show on Tuesday and a film, *Heaven Can Wait*, on Sunday.

   Do not set off restrictive modifying phrases and clauses with commas. A restrictive element restricts, or limits, the meaning of the word it follows.

   The man fidgeting in the witness box is my brother.
   The snow that was falling in Buffalo was worse than the snow here.
   We saw the film *Heaven Can Wait*; what film did you see?

6. Commas are used to set off parenthetic words and expressions—words and expressions that interrupt the sentence.

   Yes, I read the story. I did not like it, however.
   This book, I believe, is worth reading; in fact, I loved it.

7. Commas are used to set off a direct quotation that is not a grammatical part of the entire sentence.

   He replied, "Live and let live."

   When the quotation is a grammatical part of the sentence, do not use commas unless the sentence structure makes them necessary.

   He said that people should "live and let live."

8. Commas are used in dates to separate the day's name from the month, the day's number from the year, and the end of the date from the rest of the sentence.

   Friday, June 10, 1983, will be my fifteenth birthday.

9. Commas are used in street addresses to separate the street from the town or city, the town or city from the state or country, the state from the country, and the end of the address from the rest of the sentence.

   We have lived at 18 Remson Place, Yucaipa, California, for years.
   I like Paris, France, but Utah, U.S.A., is home.

10. Commas are used to set off the name of a person directly addressed.

   Paul, please come here.   Go to the store, Henrietta.

Exclamation Points (!)

An exclamation point always follows an exclamation and sometimes follows an imperative sentence.

So there you are!   Hurray!   Come here!

Italics/Underlining

1. The titles of longer works—books, longer poems, plays, films, works of art, symphonies, magazines, and newspapers—are italicized (or underlined in handwriting or typewriting). The names of ships, planes, and spacecraft are also italicized (or underlined).

   The Sun Also Rises is by Ernest Hemingway.
   I read the Philadelphia Inquirer.   When did the Titanic sink?

2. Words as words and letters as letters are italicized (or underlined).

   There are two rs in embarrassed.

Periods (.)

1. A period always follows a declarative sentence and usually follows an imperative sentence.

   The first American flag had thirteen stars.   Put the flag away.

2. Periods are used in most abbreviations. (Note: *Miss* is not an abbreviation.)

   Mrs. Mr. Ms. Dr. Sr. B.A. N.C.
   St. Ave. Blvd. U.S.A. B.C. a.m.

   Some abbreviations and acronyms (words formed with the first letters of each important word in a term) do not use periods. Official post office abbreviations accompanied by zip codes do not use periods. You can check abbreviations in your dictionary.

   NOW (National Organization of Women)   New Haven, CT 06510
   UFO (unidentified flying object)   North Huron, SD 57501

Question Marks (?)

A question mark follows an interrogative sentence.

Did you see the show last night?

Quotation Marks (" ") (' ')

1. Quotation marks are used to set off a direct quotation.

   "To track down one's past," wrote Mrs. Schultz, "is rewarding."

2. Quotation marks are used to set off the titles of stories, short poems, articles, chapters, essays, songs, TV shows, and other short works.

   Did you read Keats's poem "Ode on a Grecian Urn"?

3. Quotation marks are used to set off coined words or words intended to mean something different from what they normally mean.

   Dental floss is a good "detartaring" device.
   Our "meal" consisted of two carrot sticks and a glass of water.

4. Single quotation marks are used inside double quotation marks.

   "I read parts of 'Ode to a Nightingale,' " said Joan.

NOTE: A comma or a period *always* goes inside a closing quotation mark.
A semicolon or a colon *always* goes outside a closing quotation mark.
A question mark or an exclamation point goes either inside or outside a closing quotation mark, depending on whether or not it is part of the quotation.

   I read, "A Visit of Charity." He asked, "Where am I?"
   Jill said, "I want to go home"; I said, "Let's go later."
   Who said, "Don't fire till you see the whites of their eyes"?

Semicolons (;)

1. A semicolon is used to separate two independent, related clauses when a coordinate conjunction is not used.

   We arrived late; in fact, we missed most of the party.

2. Semicolons are used to separate items in a series when at least one element already has a comma.

   We studied *The Hairy Ape*, *Anna Christie*, and *The Iceman Cometh* by Eugene O'Neill; and *Arms and the Man* by George Bernard Shaw.

PART 3 **USAGE**

Adjectives and Adverbs

1. An adjective modifies a noun, a pronoun, or a gerund.

   Your terrible boasting has angered your loyal fans.

   An adverb or adverbial phrase tells how, how often, when, or where. Most adverbs and adverbials modify verbs.

   Grace ran quickly up the hill this morning.

   A common error that many people make is to use adjectives when they should use adverbs. Remember, adjectives do not modify verbs.

   She ran quickly (not quick).   She sings well (not good).

2. Both adjectives and adverbs can be used to show comparison. There are two degrees of comparison: comparative and superlative. Comparative degree is used to compare two items. Superlative degree is used to compare three or more items. Rules for showing comparison are as follows.

   a. For all one-syllable and some two-syllable adjectives and adverbs, add *-er* for the comparative and *-est* for the superlative.

   Carlos ran fast.
   Roy ran faster than Carlos.
   Hilda ran fastest of all

   Lin is an able skier.
   Kim is abler than Lin.
   Nina is ablest of all.

   b. For all other adjectives and adverbs, use the word *more* for the comparative and the word *most* for the superlative.

   Carlos ran quickly.
   Roy ran more quickly than Carlos.
   Hilda ran most quickly of all.

   Lin is an expert skier.
   Kim is more expert than Lin.
   Nina is most expert of all.

   c. A few adjectives and adverbs show comparative and superlative degrees by changing form completely.

	Comparative	Superlative
good, well	better	best
bad	worse	worst
little (meaning *few*)	less	least

A common error that many people make is to use a double comparative or superlative form.

Dan came more earlier than Kevin. Iris is the most prettiest girl.

Agreement

1. A present-tense verb must agree with its subject. The simple form of the verb is used with *I*, *you*, and all plural subjects. The *s* form is used with all singular subjects except *I* and *you*.

   I leave home at 6 a.m.
   You leave home at 6 a.m.
   We leave home at 6 a.m.
   The boys leave home at 6 a.m.

   She leaves home at 6 a.m.
   He leaves home at 6 a.m.
   The girl leaves home at 6 a.m.
   It leaves its nest at 6 a.m.

   Sometimes the word *Here* or *There* is used as a sentence starter. In this case, the verb agrees with the subject that follows.

   Here is your sandwich. There are apples in the refrigerator.

   For more information on present-tense verb forms, see page 122.

2. A pronoun must agree with the noun or other pronoun to which it refers.

   I know that girl. She is my friend. (She refers to girl.)
   After it was repaired, my car ran well. (It refers to car.)
   I studied the trees in the forest. They were birches. (They refers to trees.)

   For more information on pronouns, see page 121.

3. Many people make agreement errors with singular indefinite pronouns (see the list on page 121). Remember: A singular indefinite pronoun is not affected by any adjective phrase that comes after it.

   Each of the girls leaves her dirty dishes in the sink. (Do not be confused by the adjective phrase of the girls; the subject Each is singular.)
   Everyone in my classes understands his or her homework.

   A few indefinite pronouns may be either singular or plural (see the list on page 121). With these pronouns, the adjective phrases are helpful.

   Some of the food gives me indigestion. Some gives me heartburn.
   Some of the girls leave home at 6 a.m. Some leave at 7 a.m.

4. Nouns or pronouns joined by *and* form a compound expression that is plural.

   Marta and Jo leave home at six, and they arrive here at noon.

   If the expression joined by *and* names a single thing, it is singular.

   Bacon and eggs is my favorite dish. I eat it for breakfast each morning.

5. Singular nouns or pronouns joined by *or* or *nor* form a compound expression that is singular.

   Either Marta or Jo leaves her dirty dishes in the sink.

   Plural nouns or pronouns joined by *or* or *nor* form a plural expression.

   Neither the girls nor the boys leave their dirty dishes in the sink.

   You should avoid constructions in which a singular is joined to a plural by *or* or *nor*. However, the rule for such a case is that the verb or any pronoun agrees with the closer word.

   Acceptable: Neither the girls nor Granny leaves her dishes in the sink.
   Better: The girls don't leave their dishes in the sink, and neither does Granny.
   Acceptable: Either Granny or the girls leave their dishes in the sink.
   Better: Granny leaves her dishes in the sink, and so do the girls.

Comparison (See Adjectives and Adverbs on page 118.)

Dangling Modifiers (See Unit 3, page 46.)

Double Negatives

1. Using more than one negative word or contraction in a clause is considered a mistake.

   I won't go nowhere should be changed to:
   I won't go anywhere OR I will go nowhere.

2. The words *barely, hardly,* and *scarcely* are half negatives and also should not appear together with another negative word.

   They hardly have no homework should be changed to:
   They hardly have any homework.

Fragments

A sentence fragment is a group of words that, though punctuated like a sentence, does not express a complete thought.

When it rained, naturally. The girl that I met on the train.

In general, you should avoid sentence fragments in your writing. However, fragments are sometimes acceptable—in realistic dialogue, for example.

"When did you reach the beach?" "When it rained, naturally."
"Who else went with you?" "The girl that I met on the train."

Misplaced Modifiers (See Unit 3, page 46)

Negatives (See Double Negatives,page 119)

Nouns

1. A noun names a person, an animal, a place, a thing, or an idea.

   The woman raised her voice in anger.
   This morning, Nate brought the horses to the mountain.

2. A noun can be either common or proper. A proper noun is the name of a particular person, animal, place, or thing. The first letter is always capitalized (see page 113).

   Mary Rover United States World War II

   A common noun is any other noun.

   girl dog country event

3. A noun can be singular (one) or plural (more than one). The rules for spelling the plural forms of nouns follow.

   a. In most cases, the plural form is made by adding -*s* to the singular.

      boy, boys dog, dogs event, events

   b. When a singular noun ends in *ch, s, sh, x,* or *z*,add -*es* to form the plural.

      church, churches tress, tresses sash, sashes fox, foxes

   c. When a singular noun ends in a consonant plus *y*, the plural is formed by changing the *y* to *i* and adding -*es*.

      baby, babies candy, candies dictionary, dictionaries

   d. When a singular noun ends in a consonant plus *o*, the plural is sometimes formed by adding -*es*. Check your dictionary.

      tomato, tomatoes potato, potatoes cargo, cargoes

   e. When a singular noun ends in *f* or *fe*, the plural is sometimes formed by changing the *f* or *fe* to *v* and adding -*es*. Check your dictionary.

      thief, thieves knife, knives leaf, leaves

   f. Irregular plurals are formed in various ways. Whenever you are not sure, check your dictionary.

      foot, feet datum, data child, children deer, deer

4. A noun can be made into a possessive to show ownership. A singular noun is made into a possessive by adding an apostrophe (') and an s.

   the girl's bike   the box's contents   Chris's book

   To form the possessive of a plural noun that ends in s, just add an apostrophe.

   the girls' bicycles   the boxes' contents   the knives' blades

   If the plural form does not end in s, add an apostrophe and an s to form the possessive.

   the deer's antlers   the men's houses   the people's club

Plurals (See Agreement, page 118, and Nouns, page 120.)

Possession (See Nouns, page 120, and Pronouns below.)

Pronouns

1. Pronouns have subject, object, and possessive forms. Many people have difficulty using correct pronoun forms in compound constructions.
   a. Use subject pronouns for subjects of sentences or predicate nominatives (following linking verbs).

      Karen and I went to the theater.   The winners were Myron and she.
   b. Use object pronouns for objects of verbs, prepositions, or verbals.

      Beth is meeting Margaret and them for dinner. (direct object)
      Give Maurice or her the book (indirect object)
      To Bill and me, Paris was delightful. (object of a preposition)
2. Possessive pronouns, like possessive nouns, show ownership. But unlike possessive nouns, possessive pronouns do not have any apostrophes.

   My dress used to be hers.   Max's cat twisted its tail around a tree.

   A common error people make is to confuse certain possessive pronouns with contractions that they sound like.

   Its time has come. (Its is a possessive pronoun.)
   It's time to go. (It's is a contraction for it is.)
3. An indefinite pronoun refers to an unspecified person, place, or thing. Most indefinite pronouns are singular, some can be singular or plural, and a few are always plural. For agreement with indefinite pronouns, see page 119.

INDEFINITE PRONOUNS

Always Singular			Singular or Plural		Always Plural
another	everybody	no one	all	most	both
anybody	everyone	nothing	any	none	few
anyone	everything	one	enough	some	many
anything	much	other	more	such	several
each	neither	somebody			
either	nobody	someone			
		something			

Run Ons

A run-on sentence is a sentence in which two or more independent clauses are joined together without correct punctuation.

Jeff watched TV Nancy listened to the stereo.
Jeff watched TV, Nancy listened to the stereo.

The above run-on sentences could be corrected as follows:

a. Add a semicolon to show that the two independent clauses are related. (You may also add a conjunctive adverb.)

Jeff watched TV; Nancy listened to the stereo.
Jeff watched TV; however, Nancy listened to the stereo.

b. Add a coordinating conjunction between the two independent clauses.

Jeff watched TV, but Nancy listened to the stereo.

c. Add a subordinating conjunction to one of the clauses.

While Jeff watched TV, Nancy listened to the stereo.

d. If the two clauses are unrelated, make them into separate sentences.

Run on: Jeff watched TV did you do the homework?
Corrected: Jeff watched TV. Did you do the homework?

Verbs

Verbs have five forms.

a. The simple form is used for present tense with plural subjects, *I*, and *you*. (It is sometimes called the plural form.) It is also used after all helping verbs except forms of *have* and *be*.

I play. The girls play. He will play.

b. The -*s* form is the simple form plus -*s*. It is used for present tense with singular subjects (except *I* and *you*). (It is sometimes called the singular form.)

The girl plays. She plays.

The verb *be* has three present-tense forms.

I am You (or plural subjects) are It (or other singular subjects) is

c. The -*ing* form, or the present participle, is the simple form plus -*ing*. It is used after the helping verb *be* to form the progressive tenses. For spelling changes in the -*ing* form, consult your dictionary.

d. The -*ed* ending is used for both the past tense and the past participle, but these are actually different forms. The past tense -*ed* form stands alone.

He played. They played. We played. I played.

Notice that the same past-tense form is used for all subjects, except with *be*.

I was You (or plural subjects) were He (or singular subjects) was

For spelling changes in the past tense, consult your dictionary.

e. The past participle (also *-ed* ending) is used after the helping verb *have*.

I have played. She has played. I had played.

f. Irregular verbs are verbs that do not form their past tense and past participle (*-ed*) forms in the regular way. The term does not apply to mere spelling changes (*hurry* to *hurried*, for example) but to complete irregularity. Often, irregular verbs have two different forms for past tense and past participle.

I did it; I have done it.

For irregular verb forms, consult your dictionary.

NOTE: Make sure you do not confuse the simple past tense with the past participle when they are different.

Wrong: I have broke it. Right: I have broken it.

PART IV **LETTER FORMS**

1. Most business letters have six parts arranged in the following way.

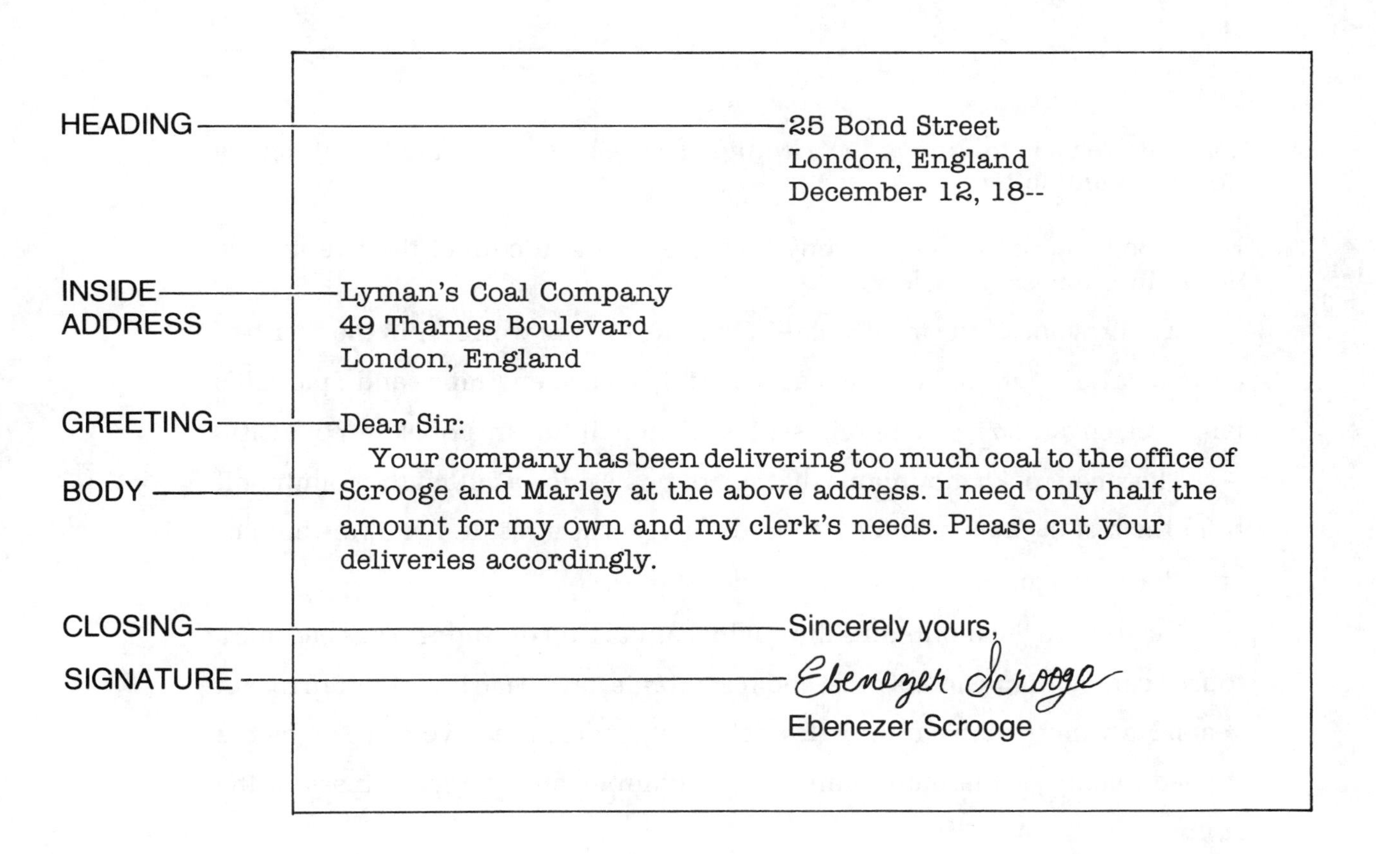

HEADING — 25 Bond Street
London, England
December 12, 18--

INSIDE ADDRESS — Lyman's Coal Company
49 Thames Boulevard
London, England

GREETING — Dear Sir:

BODY — Your company has been delivering too much coal to the office of Scrooge and Marley at the above address. I need only half the amount for my own and my clerk's needs. Please cut your deliveries accordingly.

CLOSING — Sincerely yours,

SIGNATURE — Ebenezer Scrooge
Ebenezer Scrooge

2. A colon is used following the greeting of a formal business letter.

3. Most friendly letters have five parts arranged in the following way.

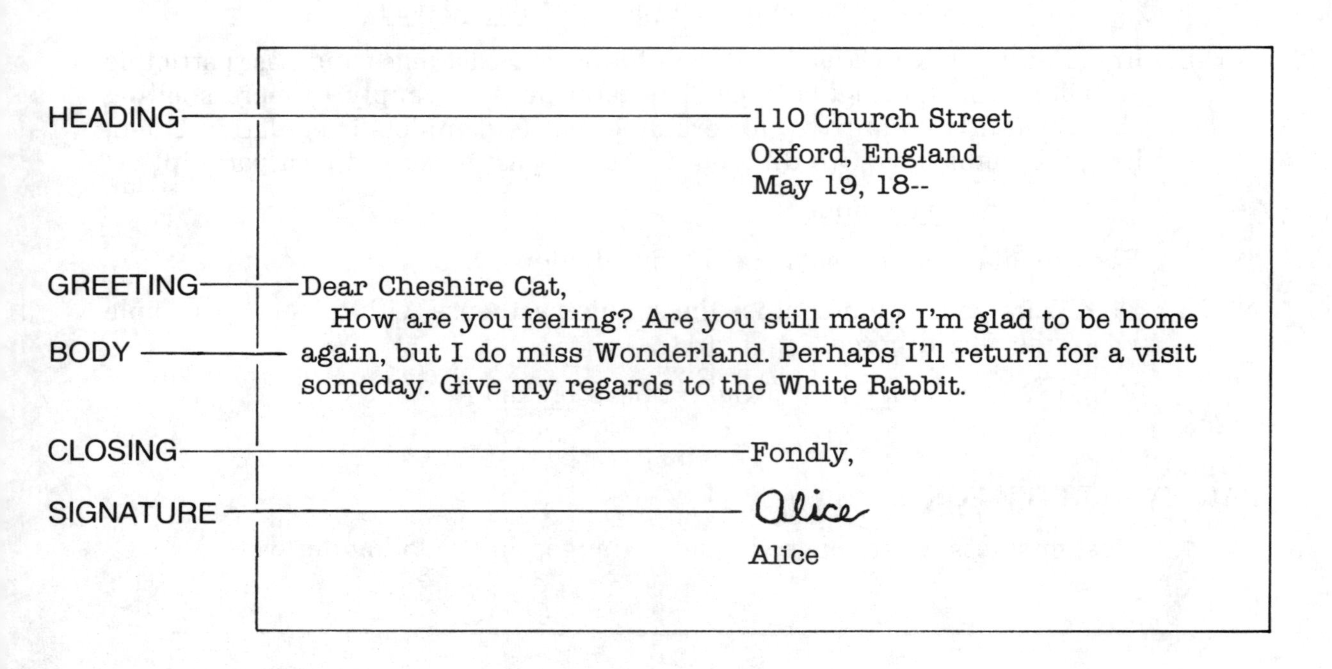

HEADING — 110 Church Street
Oxford, England
May 19, 18--

GREETING — Dear Cheshire Cat,

BODY — How are you feeling? Are you still mad? I'm glad to be home again, but I do miss Wonderland. Perhaps I'll return for a visit someday. Give my regards to the White Rabbit.

CLOSING — Fondly,

SIGNATURE — Alice
Alice

4. Commas are used following the greeting of a friendly letter, and following the closing of any letter.

A. How good a proofreader are you? Can you find and correct the twenty-five errors in the passage below?

Andorra one of the most smallest countrys in the world, is in the South of europe. It lies high in the pyranees mountains between France and Spain. It's land area covers 175 square miles—less than half the area of New York City.

The steep rocky mountains that surrounds Andorra cutted the country off from the rest of the world for hundreds of years as a result, Andorras boundaries has changed little since the Middle Ages.

Nestling in the mountains the quaint capital City of Andorra has became a tourist center. Many hotels inns, and restaurants have been built their in recent years. Now more than a million tourists visit Andorra each year. To enjoy the rugged beauty of the mountains the old churchs and the quaintness of the country.

Unit 1

Lesson 1 (pages 2–5)

A. noticed chaos there
went to field and found cow
tried to get her up
decided she might die

B. 5, 1, 2, 3, 6, 4

C. ⇨⇦ When you see this symbol, check with your teacher.

D. ⇨⇦ **E.** ⇨⇦ **F.** ⇨⇦

Lesson 2 (pages 6–9)

A. ⇨⇦

B.
I. Preparation for trip
II. Travel to faraway ______
III. Accomplishing my mission
IV. Escape from faraway ______

C, D. Subhead order may vary.
I. Preparation for trip
  A. Bought new clothes
    1. Cape
    2. Gloves
  B. Bought necessary equipment
    1. Skis
    2. Ropes
  C. Left notes for people
    1. Teachers
    2. Parents

E.
II. Travel to faraway ______
  B. Second part of the trip, from ______ to ______
III. Accomplishing my mission
  A. Arrival at the hotel
  C. My first meeting with ______
    1. How I got to see ______
    2. First impressions of ______
  D. Getting the ______
    2. How my plan almost fails
IV. Escape from ______
  A. A problem getting away

F. ⇨⇦

Lesson 3 (pages 10–13)

A. Did you underline *Last June . . . fishing?*

B. ⇨⇦ **C.** ⇨⇦

D.
1. The banging of the door reminded her of the banging of his gate.
2. She felt more kindly toward her daughter after thinking fondly of her time with her grandfather.

E. ⇨⇦

Lesson 4 (pages 14–15)

A. ⇨⇦ **B.** ⇨⇦

C. You should have underlined *One drizzly afternoon, down Main Street, After a few minutes, alongside her, on the head, happily, in vain, back home, beside her, all the way.* They tell when, where, how.

D. ⇨⇦

Unit 2

Lesson 1 (pages 18–21)

A.
1. It was no accident that Nadine was the best tuba-player in the county.
2. And there I was, transformed into a clown, me and yet not me.

B. 1. effects 2. causes

C. B 1. E 2. E 3. B 4. E 5. E 6. E 7. B 8. B 9. B 10.

D. ⇨⇦ **E.** ⇨⇦ **F.** ⇨⇦ **G.** ⇨⇦ **H.** ⇨⇦

Lesson 2 (pages 22–25)

A. The accident: The letter carrier dropped a package containing a glass aquarium and it broke.
The causes:
Mother didn't latch door.
Luis didn't keep dog inside.
Dog barked and ran out to letter carrier.
Letter carrier was upset and dropped package.

B. ⇨⇦ **C.** ⇨⇦

D.
1. A rainstorm will soon start.
2. The days will continue to grow longer until summer—June 21—comes.
3. No life as we know it exists on Planet X.
4. The animals will not survive unless something is done to give them food.
5. The rivers will become polluted. Fish will die. People will not be able to use the water for drinking.

Lesson 3 (pages 26–29)

A. ⇨⇦

B. 5 1. 1 2. 3 3. 4 4. 2 5.

C. ⇨⇦ **D.** ⇨⇦

E. Did you draw arrows between 3 and 4, 5 and 6, 6 and 7, 7 and 8, 8 and 9, 10 and 11, 11 and 12?

F. ⇨⇦

Lesson 4 (pages 30–31)

A.
1. I would love to go on the camping trip, but I hurt my leg.
2. Give me that notebook since (because) I paid for it.
3. I must clean my room before (and) I can go to the movies.
4. When (While, Because) Yoko came to visit me, I stopped doing my homework.
5. I was hot and tired, so (therefore, consequently, before, and) I drank a glass of iced tea.
6. Since (Because) Teresa's painting was the best, (therefore, consequently) it won first prize.
7. Since (Because) Walter was bored, (therefore, so) he drummed his fingers on the table.

B. Answers will vary. Here is one possibility. Early one morning there was a fire in the hospital. No one knows how it happened since there were not many people around early that morning. Because there was very little smoke, not many people saw any smoke. Neither the nurses nor the doctors smelled anything. The fire started on the first floor and spread quickly to the upper floors. The fire alarm on the first floor did not work; consequently a lot of damage was done there. When the fire engines finally arrived, the fire was soon put out.

Unit 3

Lesson 1 (pages 34–37)

A.

1.	people laughing and talking	gulls screeching
	people munching and slurping	coins jingling
		waves lapping shore
		car and boat engines
2.	briny sea	suntan lotion
	gas	clams, other food
3.	salt water	corn on the cob
	clams	ice cream
	shrimp	soft drinks
4.	sea breeze	wooden dock
	cold water	bike pedals and handlebars
	sun on your face	bags and cans
	people's hands	cold, smooth ice cream

B. ➪

C. Appearance: three men with long hair wearing cowboy shirts, jeans, and boots, two have mustaches; one woman with long hair and flower wearing a flowered blouse and long skirt. Instruments and sounds: drums beating out the tempo; guitars twanging the melody; singers harmonizing as they belt out the words; microphones amplifying the sounds.

D. ➪ **E.** ➪ **F.** ➪

Lesson 2 (pages 38–41)

A.
1. banker, merchant, manufacturer; a rich man.
2. big and loud with a metallic laugh
3. made of stretched coarse material
4. puffed head; swelled veins in temples
5. to hold eyes open and lift up eyebrows
6. an inflated balloon
7. standing up in disorder as if blown about by his boastfulness

B. ➪ **C.** ➪ **D.** ➪

Lesson 3 (pages 42–45)

A. It was Christmas Eve, dark and cold. Scrooge doesn't trust his clerk, doesn't give him much fire, and keeps him working on Christmas Eve. Scrooge seems an unkind, penny-pinching employer.

B. Appearance: glasses; wearing safari outfit, visored cap; peering through binoculars; has notebook, pencil, camera, and canteen.
Character Traits: ➪

C. ➪

D.
1. boat moored
   sails furled
   brass shone in moonlight
2. strange smell like dead roses

E. ➪ **F.** ➪

Lesson 4 (pages 46–47)

A.
1. The terrified child, lost and alone, screamed for his mother.
2. Colorful tulips and daffodils filled the garden with their perfume and beauty.
3. An enormous diamond sparkled in the center of the maroon velvet case.
4. A tiny girl struggled under the weight of a huge box wrapped in gay paper.

B.
1. The police were always after Alonzo, a known dealer in stolen goods.
2. One can of dog food a day wasn't enough for the hungry family of eight puppies.
3. The howling dog disturbed Marjorie, (who was) reading a scary mystery.
4. The vet came to see the cow that was mooing loudly in the barn.
5. Greg gave Cindy a valentine with a red heart and white lace.

Unit 4

Lesson 1 (pages 50–53)

A.
1. the airplane
2. the tricycle
3. ➪
4. ➪

B. ➪

C.

alarm	no	yes
needs outlet	no	yes
FM	no	yes
price	cheaper	more expensive
number of colors	5	2

D.
1. Did you underline the first sentence?
2. number of gears; weight; price
3. less, less effort, more expensive, better, higher, more gears, lighter

E. ➪ **F.** ➪ **G.** ➪

Lesson 2 (pages 54–57)

A.
1. players
2. birth and death
3. ➪(son or daughter, sister or brother, student, etc.)

B.
1. In life we are taught to fight with each other.
2. You might say it's confusing; it's not always neat and orderly; some things get broken.
3. Events are repeated; we have the same feelings and thoughts at different times.

C.

1. M	3. S	5. M
2. S	4. M	6. S

D. ➪ **E.** ➪

F.
1. Night
2. She wears garments and goes through halls.

G.
1. lonely as a cloud; continuous as the stars
2. daffodils, waves, the poet's heart

3. He changes from pensive to pleasure-filled because he remembers the loveliness of the daffodils.

H.

Lesson 3 (page 58–61)

A. 1. a snake
2. (a tree) arms and legs like twigs
3. Aunt Alice

B. C.

D. Caesar is the shortest boy without glasses.
Eric is the twin with fewer freckles.
Hiram is the shorter boy with glasses.
Irving is the shorter, heavy boy.

E. 1. Lem was lazy. He hardly ever moved.
2. Juanita was energetic. She bustled about, cleaning and fixing, and was never still.
3. Juanita, Lem, Lem, Juanita

F.

Lesson 4 (pages 62–63)

A. 1. exceptional (able)
2. considerable (ate)
3. continuous (al)
4. frightful
5. impressive (ible)
6. mischievous
7. critical
8. dusty

B. C.

Unit 5

Lesson 1 (pages 66–69)

A. Objective Statements
Florida was discovered in 1513 by Ponce de Léon.
The 5,000-square-mile preserve contains a multitude of tropical plants and animals.
It is here that the world's first moon flight was launched in 1969.
Subjective Statements
The other sentences—1, 3, 4, 6, 8—are subjective.

B. Answers may be similar to these:
2. I'm angry that the tax rate rose last year.
3. I love citrus fruit.
4. Willie Mays was a wonderful ballplayer.
5. The Beatles were a great group.
6. I hate dentists.

C. Answers may be similar to these:
1. Most cola drinks contain caffeine.
2. Hawaii is our fiftieth state.
3. The Concorde can fly faster than the speed of sound.
4. Turnips contain vitamins A, B complex, and C.
5. There are twenty-six major league baseball teams.

D. 1. O 2. S 3. O 4. S 5. S 6. O

E. F.

Lesson 2 (pages 70–73)

A. 1. newspaper
2. encyclopedia, almanac
3. dictionary
4. book of quotations
5. encyclopedia, who's who, biography
6. textbook, encyclopedia
7. almanac
8. textbook, encyclopedia
9. professional journal
10. who's who, biography, encyclopedia

B. 1. b 2. a 3. b 4. b 5. a

C. D. E.

Lesson 3 (pages 74–77)

A. g 1. h 2. b 3. c 4. e 5. a 6. f 7. d 8.

B. C.

Lesson 4 (pages 78–79)

A.

B. Answers may be similar to these:
1. toys, bikes
2. popcorn, candy
3. farms, houses, office buildings
4. The Women's Club, Ann and Jeff, my cousins
5. lion, eagle

C. Answers may be similar to these:
1. whisper, shout, mumble, orate
2. glance, ogle, stare, view
3. paint, repair, write, carve

D. Answers may be similar to these:
1. whimpered, moaned
2. drifted, floated
3. gulped, gobbled
4. glared, frowned

E.

Unit 6

Lesson 1 (pages 82–85)

A.

Formal Diction	Informal Diction
honor, presence, reception, ceremony, R.S.V.P.	bash, dogs, burgers, pop, buck, pad

B. C.

D. Your dialogue should be similar to this:
Jim: I'm going to grab some lunch at Ye Old Tea Shoppe at noon today. Like to join me?
Bill: Sure. Thanks a lot. Let's go downtown later. I have a big date at two.
Jim: OK. I'll be glad to go with with you.

E. Your translation should be similar to this:
I got so tired mowing the lawn that I didn't see that soda bottle that badly damaged the power mower. Then my father wanted to take five dollars from my allowance to pay for the damage. When I talked back, he told me I couldn't go out nor could I borrow his car for Bennie's party. I said, "Dad, how can you do that? You know I can't get to the party without a car."
"Don't be silly," he said. "Bennie's apartment is only 4 blocks away. You can walk."

Lesson 2 (pages 86–89)

A. which candidate to vote for
which restaurant to eat in
which bone to chew

B. C.
D. Here are some sample arguments:
1. Pro: Everyone should have a basic education.
   Con: Some people learn better in a job situation than in school.
2. Pro: I can work to change club rules.
   Con: I don't believe in excluding people.
3. Pro: With interest, it would grow and provide something to fall back on.
   Con: My family and I have certain needs that I would like to take care of.

E.

Lesson 3 (pages 90–93)

A.
B. Curly's letter is more effective because it states precise facts about the problem and suggests a solution—a refund.
C. D. E.

Lesson 4 (pages 94–95)

A. 1. Since the mud was too soft, the man kept falling down and dissolving into the earth.
2. Then using wood, God made another man who did not fall down or dissolve.
3. This man, who was stiff and inflexible, stood there and looked stupid.
4. Then taking corn meal dough, God shaped a man and baked him firm in the sun.
5. This pliant, golden brown man had the shape that all men took forever after.

B. Answers may be similar to this:

A dog who was looking for a place for an afternoon nap jumped into an ox's manger. The dog lay there upon the cozy straw. Soon the ox returned from its work and came up to the manger, wanting to eat some straw. The dog was awakened from its slumber. In a rage, the dog stood up and barked at the ox. As the ox came near, the dog tried to bite it. Giving up hope of getting at the straw, the ox went away muttering, "People often will not let others enjoy things they cannot enjoy themselves."

Unit 7

Lesson 1 (pages 98–101)

A. B. C. D.

Lesson 2 (pages 102–105)

A. TP 1. FP 2. FP 3. TP 4. FP 5.
B. C. D.

Lesson 3 (pages 106–109)

A.
B. Your dialogue may begin like this:

ALICE (to Cat in tree): What sort of people live about here?

CAT: In that direction *(waving right paw)* lives a Hatter; and in that direction *(waving other paw)* lives a March Hare. Visit either you like: they're both mad.

Lesson 4 (pages 110–111)

A. Answers may be similar to these:
1. The couple danced wildly at the disco until 3 A.M.
2. After the spaceship went off without her, the astronaut had to make her home on the strange planet. She remembered she had some seed packets in her back pocket; therefore, she decided to plant the seeds.
3. The bored audience squirmed through the dull speech.
4. Ludwig swept up the broken vase which was shattered into a thousand pieces. Smiling broadly, Aunt Matilda bought a new vase.
5. The room which had been thoroughly searched was a complete mess. Paco felt disturbed as he looked at the chaos.
6. The mountain climbers spied tiny villages nestled in the valley below.
7. My little brother made pancakes for breakfast. They didn't taste very good, however, since they were burned on one side and not cooked enough on the other side.

B. Answers may be similar to this:
The plane was flying smoothly. Suddenly the plane lurched as the pilot slumped over. The plane was spinning wildly until the co-pilot took the controls. Then the wild spinning stopped as the plane flew smoothly and straight again.

Handbook (page 124)

A. Andorra, one of the ~~most~~ smallest countries in the world, is in the south of Europe. It lies high in the Pyranees Mountains between France and Spain. ~~It's~~ Its land area covers 175 square miles—less than half the area of New York City.

The steep, rocky mountains that surround Andorra cut~~ted~~ the country off from the rest of the world for hundreds of years. As a result, Andorra's boundaries have changed little since the Middle Ages.

Nestling in the mountains, the quaint capital city of Andorra has become a tourist center. Many hotels, inns, and restaurants have been built ~~their~~ there in recent years. Now more than a million tourists visit Andorra each year to enjoy the rugged beauty of the mountains, the old churches, and the quaintness of the country.

Post-Test Answers; pg 16

1. 2, 5, 3, 4, 1, 6
2. I. Purposes for Bicycles
   - A. Transportation
   - B. Pleasure and Relaxation

   II. Bicycle Maintenance
   - A. Gear and chain repair
     1. 10-speed bicycles
     2. 3-speed bicycles
   - B. Fixing flat tires
3. Answers will vary. Be sure adverbs answer the questions in parentheses.
4. Check to see that except for the flashback the events in the paragraphs proceed in a logical sequence. Note whether the flashback adds meaning and interest to the paragraph.

Post-Test Answers; pg 32

1. We really worked hard to make the house look great.
2. a cause
3. b
   d
   a
   c
4. Conjunctions used may vary. Here are some examples:
   - a. Our balloon has a rip in it; therefore we must walk across the jungle.
   - b. We can't buy an elephant because our rhinos take up too much room at home.
   - c. Since the shop was giving away ice cream, children lined up for two blocks.
5. C
   R
   C
   R
6. Make sure that the students' stories actually resolve the stated conflicts. Check that the cause-and-effect chain of events in each story proceeds logically. You might want to ask the students to underline the cause-and-effect words that they have used.

Post-Test Answers; pg 48

1. a. Accept any realistic details, such as size; shape; color of hair, skin, eyes; posture; voice; gestures.
   b. Accept any superpowers, such as extraordinary strength, great intelligence, special vision, hearing, mobility.
2. a. Accept any detail that changes the setting to a different time or place, such as an unearthly animal or atmosphere.
   b. Accept any detail that seems suspicious or obviously out of place, such as strange shadows or noises, criminal activity, or boarded up windows.
3. a. Under the bed, Claire found her good hat, squashed and dusty.
   b. With a loud noise, the giant crashed into Mother's lovely antique china.
   c. Flying at an altitude of 2000 feet, we thought the lake looked tiny.
4. Be sure the students have written three paragraphs and organized them as directed. Check for topic sentences and supporting details. You may want to have students underline the adjectives they have used.

Post-Test Answers; pg 64

1. Answers may be similar to these:

Features	*Clothesline*	*Dryer*
cost	cheaper	more expensive
convenience	less convenient	more convenient
energy efficient	more efficient	less efficient

2. S a. M b.
   P c. M d.
   M e. P f.

   If students express an interest in the writers quoted, you may wish to give them the following brief information and have them do further research:
   Theodore Roosevelt, American president
   Moira O'Neill, Irish poet
   Alexander Smith, Scottish poet
   Henry Thoreau, American poet and essayist
   William Service, Canadian poet
   Emily Dickinson, American poet
3. Answers will vary. Here are examples:.
   - a. The stew was so bitter and greasy I couldn't swallow a bite.
   - b. The military band's music sounds so exciting that I want to start marching.
   - c. Our new English teacher can make 200-year-old plays and poems come alive in our classroom.
4. Check that the paragraph begins with a topic sentence and ends with a concluding sentence. Be sure they have listed three similarities and three differences. You may wish to have the students underline the adjectives they used to compare and contrast.

Post-Test Answers; pg 80

1. S a. O d.
   O b. O e.
   S c.
2. c. It is more narrow than a. It can be researched, whereas b is merely subjective.
3. d
   c
   b
   a
4. Answers will vary. Here are some samples:
   a. typewriter, computer, toaster
   b. doll, jack-in-the-box, football
   c. stroll, amble, plod
   d. giggle, guffaw, roar
5. You may want to allow the students to choose another topic to write about. In any event, make sure the first paragraph contains only objective statements and the second paragraph only subjective statements. Watch for sentences that combine objective and subjective statements.

Post-Test Answers; pg 96

1. Answers should be similar to this:
   Dan and I kept asking Mom to pay for the movies, but she wouldn't give us money until we cleaned up our room. The room was very messy and was bothering her a great deal. We worked very hard but finished the job.
2. Answers will vary. Here are two:
   Pro: It is important to learn to work with others as part of a team.
   Con: Many students have little interest in sports and should not be forced to play.
3. Here is one revision:
   The hungry fox wanted some grapes, but they were on a high vine. The fox jumped for the grapes again and again. Since he couldn't reach them, he gave up and said, "Those grapes are sour and bitter."
4. Check that students have begun both of their paragraphs with topic sentences. Also check that both pro and con arguments are logical.

Post-Test Answers; pg 96

1. Answers will vary. Both Jack and Jill will probably be hurt or upset. Jill may blame Jack. Dame Dobb may describe Jack's would or recount the children's description of the accident.
2. Answers should be similar to this:
   "You aren't cross, I suppose, Peggotty, are you?" David asked, after a minute.
   He really thought she was, she had been so short with him; but he was quite mistaken; for she laid aside her work, and opening her arms wide, took his curly head within them, and gave it a good squeeze.
3. MARCH HARE *(earnestly):* Take some more tea.
   ALICE *(offended):* "Ive had nothing yet, so I can't take more.
   HATTER: You mean you can't take less. It's very easy to take more than nothing.
4. Here is one example:
   The huge spaceship was cigar-shaped. When it landed, creatures with strangely glowing skulls rushed out. Two teenagers watched them from a nearby house.
5. Check to see that the students have followed the correct form for the genre they have chosen. Encourage the students to revise their work.